PREACHING THE THEOLOGY OF THE CROSS

Sermons and Worship Ideas for Lent and Easter

PETER L. STEINKE

AUGSBURG Publishing House • Minneapolis

In appreciation for three teachers
who have helped me along the way
with encouragement and enlightenment . . .

Harry G. Coiner
Sara Little
✝ Thomas C. Campbell ✝

PREACHING THE THEOLOGY OF THE CROSS

Contents

Preface

The purpose of this book is to help pastors and congregations prepare for the Lenten season and the celebration of Easter. Ideas and suggestions are provided for both preaching and worship. At the same time, this book can be used either as an introduction to or a review of Luther's "theology of the cross." As we approach 1983—the 500th anniversary of Luther's birth—it is appropriate to place Luther's *theologia crucis* in the context of his favored mode of expression, the proclaimed word in the midst of the congregation.

This book could be used in several ways. A pastor may use it in preparation for Lent and Easter, a group of pastors could use it in a joint study or at a retreat setting, or a pastor and a congregational worship committee might work together in planning sermons and services. A fourth possibility is converting the content into a series of Bible studies. The book was originally prepared for a pastors' pre-Lenten retreat. Pastors may reprint the responsive readings found at the end of the book in their service bulletins without obtaining permission from the publisher.

The "theology of the cross" theme is especially pertinent to the Lent and Easter season of the church year. However, the theme is hardly seasonal. The series of sermons and worship ideas could also be fitted into other seasons. "Seeing God's Face from Behind" could commence the Epiphany season, culminating with "Glory, Glory, Hallelujah" on Transfiguration Sunday. The theme would also be suitable during the Sundays of the Pentecost season, especially near Reformation Day, peaking with the proposed Easter sermon on the Sunday closest to All Saints Day. Yet another variation might be to have the same final sermon on Christ the King, the last Sunday of the church year.

Regardless of how you choose to use this book, I hope it enables you to present the gospel of Jesus Christ in all its folly and foolishness, paradox and scandal, power and primacy, so that the people of God may live, according to Luther's words, "in the bare confidence in his mercy."

Grateful appreciation is due Claudia Scholl, who patiently typed the manuscript and retyped it as I revised it. I am indebted to several who read the manuscript and offered suggestions: David Truemper, Norman Fintel, David Lange, Edward Mahnke, and Carl Heckmann.

Dallas, Texas
Ash Wednesday, 1982

Introduction

On April 25, 1518 an assembly of Augustinians met at Heidelberg, Germany. Luther's *Ninety-Five Theses,* posted some six months beforehand, had stirred cries of protest. Leo X asked for the assembly through the established channels of Luther's order, the Augustinians. In preparation for the disputation, Luther wrote 28 theological and 12 philosophical theses. These are commonly known as the "Heidelberg Disputation of 1518." Theses 18-24 contain Luther's "theology of the cross" in explicit contrast to what Luther calls the "theology of glory":

18. It is certain that man must utterly despair of his own ability before he is prepared to receive the grace of Christ.
19. That person does not deserve to be called a theologian who looks upon the invisible things of God as though they were clearly perceptible in those things which have actually happened [Rom. 1:20].
20. He deserves to be called a theologian, however, who comprehends the visible and manifest things of God seen through suffering and the cross.
21. A theologian of glory calls evil good and good evil. A theologian of the cross calls the thing what it actually is.

22. That wisdom which sees the invisible things of God in works as perceived by man is completely puffed up, blinded, and hardened.
23. The law brings the wrath of God, kills, reviles, accuses, judges, and condemns everything that is not in Christ [Rom. 4:15].
24. Yet that wisdom is not of itself evil, nor is the law to be evaded; but without the theology of the cross man misuses the best in the worst manner.[1]

Luther summarized his theses in the statement: "The cross puts everything to the test." [2] On the basis of these words of Luther, Heinrich Bornkamm could say that Luther made the theology of the cross "the cornerstone on which minds divide and go their different ways." It is a matter of where one *begins*—with the theology of glory or with the theology of the cross. The starting point is crucial; it determines one's understanding and the direction in which one proceeds. Walther von Loewenich remarked, for instance, that the theology of the cross is "a principle of Luther's entire theology." Though Lutherans may nod in full assent, von Loewenich spoke a word of caution:

And now it must be said: While the Lutheran church has clung faithfully to the 'for the sake of Christ' *(propter Christum)* it surrendered Luther's theology of the cross all too quickly. The theology of glory that Luther opposed has made a triumphal entry also into his church. One occasionally wonders whether the doctrine concerning the cross has not even been forced to pay tribute to this theology of glory.[3]

I am not about to argue von Loewenich's contention. I cite it merely to create an awareness of how easily we can slip into the theology of glory, regardless of one's Lutheran identity.

The theology of glory *begins* from below and proceeds to above, from the visible to the invisible, from the human to the divine. For example, the theology of glory *begins* from the order and beauty of creation or from a great event of history and then points to the spiritual power behind it. God is seen to be manifest from his works. Luther called this a process of deduction. But Luther insisted that God is hidden in suffering. God reveals himself not through "the best and the brightest," but rather through weak and foolish things, through his "opposite," the very event that apparently denies him. We see God's glory in the place where to all human appearances there is no glory. At the center of Luther's understanding is the cross of Jesus Christ, where we comprehend "the visible and manifest things of God seen through suffering and the cross."

Why should the cross, crucifixion, suffering, weakness, shame, humility, trouble, anguish, darkness, and foolishness be the focus of God's glory? Why should not the bright and prosperous features of life be the visible evidence of God's invisible power? Luther responds, "Let God be God." That is, the matter pertains to God's mystery and holiness. He will be who he will be. From another vantage point, however, Luther makes a few suggestions about the "why" of God's "how." The cross puts an end to every human attempt to take the *initiative* in finding God, whether through experience, achievement, sight, emotion, or will. The cross puts to the test any and every human insinuation of "seeing" God. It is not possible to have God in full view and with complete certainty. This is merely an expression of human fear and desire. Moreover, the creature who loves glory and the glamor of human work projects this onto the very essence of God. Humanity puts God at the mercy of human values. God becomes a glorious production of human deduction—scarcely a God of freedom, humiliation, revelation, or initiative.

Why does God reveal himself through suffering? One reason, according to Luther, is our need to be purged of sin, the need of the proud to be humbled. Suffering and humiliation allow faith to trust the sufficiency of God's grace. The worst kind of trouble is to have no trouble. Trouble keeps faith in motion— hoping, trusting, and loving. "The cross puts everything to the test." Nonetheless, Luther rejects suffering itself as being a good work or another deduction of God's presence. Luther would not boast of his own cross (suffering and humiliation) but rather of God's grace in the cross of the believer. Suffering is not redemptive. Yet it opens the door to the question of redemption.

Let us apply the theology of the cross to a few common and popular points of view. In the life of prayer, for example, a person may deduce a connection between *petition* and *answer*. The person identifies some event or behavior as God's direct, visible answer to a personal request. Even though the event or word could be coincidental or accidental, the individual nevertheless attributes it to God matter-of-factly. Indeed God does respond to our faithful seeking, knocking, and asking. But prayer is uttered with the "Amen"—"Let it be according to your will." It is therefore unnecessary to single out an answer for a specific petition. Trust implies a certain inability to see or comprehend. Trust relates to God's promise that in his graciousness he will hear us, forgive us, empower us, heal us, and transform us, somehow and some way. God's gracious promise is sufficient, and it is perfect in our weakness. According to the theology of the cross, our certainty about how God will act in a particular instance is not great. Trust connotes a measure of risk and courage, a letting be and a letting go. Our own certainty of God will never make the faithfulness of God more certain. God's graciousness is *there*. We cannot cause it, affect it, change it, or modify it. Hence, Luther interprets Rom. 8:26—"Likewise the Spirit helps us in our weakness; for we do not know how to pray as we ought, but the Spirit himself intercedes for us with sighs too deep for words"—with a striking comment: "It is not a bad sign, but a very good one, if things turn out contrary to our requests. Just as it is not a good sign if everything turns out favorably to our requests." [4] Certainly if God can conceal himself in the cross and suffering, he can also hide his gracious response to our faithful prayers. To discern his promise in precise form in personal events is not only unnecessary but also an example of seeking to deduce his glory. "Let it be!"

There are, to be sure, a multitude of ways through which we

actually seek God's glory, whether consciously, unconsciously, or semiconsciously. One often expects direct and visible dividends for far more than prayers: volunteer time, tithes, willful delays of gratification, worship experiences, and so forth. Besides such personal pieties, the theology of glory undergirds much popular religious thought. "God wants you to be rich," intones a speaker. This is an attempt to arrogate to the human side exactly what God *wills*. Conspicuous consumption becomes a work of God, a sure sign of God's glory. The gospel of success is rivaled only by the gospel of health—from "faith healing" to "mind-cure." Newer rivals to the wealth and health "deductions" are "growth" and "enthusiasm." A criticism common to all these modern theologies of glory is *triumphalism*. Illustrious and prosperous results prove the magnificence of God. The effects—miracles, signs, excitement, successes—justify the cause, God himself. There is a certain grim existentialism within the theology of the cross. Still, we are not sour-faced saints who discount divine blessings and gifts with jaundiced eyes. Success, winning, achievement, positive thoughts, happiness, and euphoria bear positive notes. But we understand them as human standards and affections. We become wary about them for the same reason Luther did with regard to good works, namely, the false opinions we attach to them. They prove nothing about the *character* of God. In fact, they can pervert the message of the cross, delivering a "cheap grace." The triumphalistic theologies of glory fail precisely in their modification of grace from a means of God to reveal his promises to an end which proves his majesty. We live by the promises of God and not by our own speculation about him or our own good fortunes. The theology of glory elevates human needs above God's challenges. It describes faith as a payoff rather than a cost. Sometimes the glory is part of a bloodless religion of mind over heart (dogmatic proofs). Sometimes it is a mindless religion of heart over mind (enthusiastic states). Luther rejected the theology of glory because of its starting point—the human mind, will, experience, or heart—which is forever looking for the naked God. In contrast, Luther says, the genesis of faith rises from the promise of God hidden in the cross and suffering. Heinrich Bornkamm comments:

Luther's concept of faith has nothing in common with any attempt to create strength and courage within ourselves by our own efforts, such as "positive thinking," nor is it related to a psychological condition of confidence which can exist without an object of trust and apart from a personal relationship. Faith exists only as a response to God's word. The word alone gives it its basis and content. This word is the word of "promise," that is, of the gospel.[5]

Alongside our personal pieties we should note the prevalence of the theology of glory in history, as human beings have incessantly sought to have God on their own terms or at their beck and call. Consider this partial list from the Scriptures:

- Adam and Eve and the tree of the knowledge of good and evil ("be like God")
- the comforters of Job
- the golden calf
- the railing thief on the cross
- the temptations of Christ
- the parable of the two sons and the reaction of the elder brother
- the Pharisees seeking signs
- the disputing disciples and the seat at the head of the table
- the parable of the publican and Pharisee praying in the temple
- the thinning of the crowds as Jesus set his face toward Jerusalem
- Nathanael's statement, "Can anything good come out of Nazareth?" (John 1:46)
- Dives (the rich man) in Hades, requesting a sign for his living relatives
- Thomas and his encounter with the resurrected Jesus
- the rich young ruler's statement, "All these I have observed from my youth" (Luke 18:21).
- the transfiguration and Peter's statement, "Master, it is well that we are here; let us make three booths . . ." (Luke 9:33).
- the Pharisees' statement, "This man is not from God, for he does not keep the sabbath" (John 9:16).
- Peter's rebuke of his Lord when Jesus said he must suffer

12

Finally, the theology of the cross, in contrast with normal standards and insights, can only be stated by means of paradoxes. Several authors have captured the paradoxical nature of the cross with book titles such as *A Severe Mercy* (Sheldon Vanauken), *The Wounded Healer* (Henri Nouwen), and *The Magnificent Defeat* (Frederick Buechner). God has sometimes been called our "beloved enemy" or the "near other." The Christian life is a paradox of finding through losing.

The cross tests everything! And the way of the cross is love, not power; suffering, not achievement; humility, not glory. shame, not honor; foolishness, not wisdom. Nothing is "worth comparing with the glory that is *to be revealed*" (Rom. 8:18; italics added). Yet "we are God's children now; it does not yet appear what we shall be, but we know that when he appears we shall be like him, for we shall see him as he is" (1 John 3:2). The best we can hope for in the present is the comfort of Jesus Christ, who suffered, was crucified, died, and was buried. He reveals the Father—not the stars or the sun, the great kingdoms or grand masters, the prosperous times or happy moments. The glory to be made manifest, with which nothing now compares, is seeing him "as he is." This glory is not a deduction, but rather a *revelation*. God is revealing himself to us now, in a paradoxical way, and will later reveal himself so that we will see fully, even as the cross assures us that we are fully understood and loved.

A brief comparison

theology of glory	*theology of the cross*
"... show me thy glory" (Exod. 33:18).	"... you cannot see my face; for man shall not see me and live" (Exod. 33:20).
"... show us the Father" (John 14:8).	"He who has seen me has seen the Father" (John 14:9).
1. knows God from his works	1. knows God from his sufferings
2. knows God directly in his obvious power and glory	2. knows God precisely where he has hidden himself, in his suffering and weakness
3. *notitia* (knowledge)	3. *fiducia* (trust)
4. majesty of God	4. grace of God
5. deductive • comprehends God in thought • moves from the visible to the invisible • good works • power and majesty • proof	5. inductive • certainty of God's love only in suffering • from darkness to light • suffering • weakness and foolishness • hiddenness

summary

"For where man's strength ends, God's strength begins.... For where man's strength begins, God's strength ends" (Martin Luther).[6]

A longer comparison

theology of glory

1. visible
2. God manifest from his works
3. directly
4. God in his naked majesty
5. glory
6. God in heaven
7. majesty
8. God found in the bright and the good
9. works
10. the naked God
11. see only wrath and trouble
12. the God of power and justice
13. empirically obvious
14. the vagabond God
15. wisdom
16. sight
17. mighty victory
18. ethical achievement
19. self-confident activism
20. speculation
21. God in himself
22. protection
23. what is
24. light
25. God apart from his word
26. certainty
27. all or nothing
28. *because* of experience
29. deductive
30. creation
31. majestic nature
32. triumph
33. from below to above
34. noble thoughts

theology of the cross

1. invisible
2. God hidden in his sufferings
3. indirectly
4. God clothed in his promise
5. humility
6. God in the man Christ
7. shame
8. God hidden in darkness
9. suffering
10. God crucified and hidden
11. God's grace hidden under trouble
12. the God of love and suffering
13. hidden under its opposite
14. the identifiable God
15. folly
16. faith ("things not seen")
17. ignominious defeat
18. call to suffering
19. humility
20. trust
21. God in relationship to human beings
22. danger
23. what will be
24. darkness
25. God bound to his word
26. *Anfechtung*
27. doubt as part of faith
28. *in spite of* experience
29. inductive
30. cross
31. humanity, weakness, foolishness
32. trial
33. God's initiative
34. crucified Christ

THE THEOLOGY OF THE CROSS IN NINE BIBLICAL TEXTS

- The following nine presentations deal with the theology of the cross based on scriptural texts.

- None of the nine presentations is intended to be a "canned" sermon in the sense that it is to be preached in its existing form.

- All of the presentations combine both explanation and proclamation, insight and persuasion, storytelling and "forth-telling," exposition and exhortation, study notes and announcements.

- The reader is invited to add "local color"—personal testimony, individual reflection, and particular passions in order to shape the final form of the proclamation.

- To impress upon hearers the core truth of the theology of the cross, several basic ideas, phrases, and words are repeated.

Moses said to the Lord, "See, thou sayest to me, 'Bring up this people' but thou hast not let me know whom thou wilt send with me. Yet thou hast said, 'I know you by name, and you have also found favor in my sight.' Now therefore, I pray thee, if I have found favor in thy sight, show me now thy ways, that I may know thee and find favor in thy sight. Consider too that this nation is thy people." And he said, "My presence will go with you, and I will give you rest." And he said to him, "If thy presence will not go with me, do not carry us up from here. For how shall it be known that I have found favor in thy sight, I and thy people? Is it not in thy going with us, so that we are distinct, I and thy people, from all other people that are upon the face of the earth?"

And the Lord said to Moses, "This very thing that you have spoken I will do; for you have found favor in my sight, and I know you by name." Moses said, "I pray thee, show me thy glory." And he said, "I will make all my goodness pass before you, and will proclaim before you my name 'The Lord'; and I will be gracious to whom I will be gracious, and will show mercy on whom I will show mercy. But," he said, "you cannot see my face for man shall not see me and live." And the Lord said, "Behold, there is a place by me where you shall stand upon the rock; and while my glory passes by I will put you in a cleft of the rock, and I will cover you with my hand until I have passed by; then I will take away my hand, and you shall see my back; but my face shall not be seen."

EXODUS 33:12-33

SEEING GOD'S FACE FROM BEHIND

The backside view

We want easy answers. We are tired of prolonged drifting, endless debating, and self-doubting. Clear-throated voices that solve our problems and put aside our questions draw immense attention, whether they are positive thinkers or magical helpers, preachers or politicians, faith healers or soothsayers. Away with confusion! We want to be cleansed of uncertainty. What charms us most is ABC advice and hocus-pocus chants. Straight and simple: what is right and who is wrong? If only we could have simple solutions, we could rivet our hopes to them. If only we could have clear enemies, we could blame our troubles on them. We want easy answers.

A strange, strange story in the book of Exodus suddenly becomes important. For there we find a great biblical character, no less than Moses, seeking the same clear certainty that we want today. Look at the situation. Moses had been on Mount Sinai for a long time. Irritated and confused, the people of Israel built the notorious golden calf. God's anger smoldered to the point that He told Moses, "To your descendants I will give it," that is, the land of promise. As for the people, they would be blotted dry from God's book. On the basis of Moses' intercession, however, God forgave the people and promised to lead them to the land: "My presence will go with you, and I will give you rest." Beset by the troublesome events, no doubt, Moses became somewhat less than certain. He hankered for added assurances, saying, "For how shall it be known that I have found favor in thy sight, I and thy people. Is it not in thy going with us, so that we are distinct, I and thy people, from all other people that are upon the face of the earth?" The Lord reassured Moses—"This very thing that you have spoken I will do." Moses must have been from Missouri. He continued, "Show me thy glory." Even then, we stand amazed that God's patience was not unduly tested. Moses wanted absolute certainty. "Show me!" "Prove it!" "Settle it once and for all." "Explain it!" "Convince me." "Make your best case for it!" Moses desperately sought to see God in his full majesty and power. No doubts. No questions. Nothing left to the imagination. Obviously, though, God drew the line, forbidding Moses to see his face, "for man shall not see me and live." Finally the strangest thing of all happened. God said to Moses:

"I will make all my goodness pass before you, and will proclaim before you my name 'The Lord' . . . 'I will be gracious to whom I will be gracious, and will show mercy on whom I will show mercy. . . . Behold, there is a place by me where you shall stand upon the rock; and while my glory passes by I will put you in a cleft of the rock, and I will cover you with my hand until I have passed by; then I will take away my hand, and you shall see my back; but my face shall not be seen . . ." [Exod 33:19-23].

Strange, isn't it? No glory, just a name and the backside of God? It is a story of seeing God's face from behind. And you guessed it—the look from behind is not full-blown and plain as pie. The full picture of God is up for grabs; it is only partial, a rear view, a quick glance. We, not satisfied with stingy solutions and half-knowledge, find this God a bit strange, giving but a promise, a name, a backside view.

Seeking God's glory

We want to see God's glory all the more if we want easy answers. For instance, we marvel at the beauty of the Rockies, jeweled in green pine and cut stone. Then we insist that the sheer beauty is no accident. "There has to be," we argue, "a God who created it all." Some of you will recognize this as the "first cause" proof of God's existence. But any deduction from the beauty of the visible world to the existence of an invisible God is too simple. Beauty itself merely leads us to the conclusion that God is an ingenious architect. Instead the psalmist gasps in wonder, "the heavens are telling the glory of God" [Ps. 19:1]. All we can conclude is that God's sense of design is magnificent. But the breathtaking view of the Rockies does not inform us about the *character* of God, his compassion, or the *mighty acts* of God, his salvation. Visible nature has no message concerning God's design and purpose for human beings. Any attempt on our part to base our faith in God on visible beauty is an attempt to make God dependent on our appreciation of that beauty. So Luther contends that God wants to be known nowhere but in his word—nowhere but in the gospel, the promise, his Son, our Lord, Jesus Christ.

Or we can be, as we often say, "swept off our feet" by some great event in our lives—a huge success, an unexpected gift, a new love—left speechless, convinced that God's work in the event was great and mighty. Once again, we come upon an easy answer, one that tells us nothing more than God is a God of incredible power. Some will recognize this as the "prime mover" proof for God's existence. It too depends on a simple deduction, proceeding from a visible event to an invisible God. In the New Testament, moreover, miracles arouse awe, not proof-pure solutions. Miracles leave the beholders wondrously puzzled. Jesus chided those who looked for signs and wonders. In the miracle story of the blind man who was given his sight, the disciples asked Jesus who had sinned. Was it the man's father or his mother?

Jesus replied, neither one. It was not a simple *cause* (sin) and *effect* (blindness) matter. The man was blind so that the glory of God might be made manifest. Miracles *reveal*. They are not primarily proofs. Whoever has eyes to see, let him see.

In both cases—beauty and power—human beings provide the starting point and we move from the visible to the invisible. "Show me thy glory!" But human reason is always partial and subject to blind spots. Eye has not yet seen what God has prepared for those who love him.

Another way we try to see God's glory is by determining his will. Some people need to point to certain events as God's answers to prayer, and this in spite of saying "Amen!"—so shall it be according to God's will. Prayer is letting go, trusting in God's will. How unnecessary it is to prove either the prayer or God, pointing to this or that as God's answer. Luther scorns such unfaithfulness:

Why, if he had to answer everybody's questions he would be a most wretched God. Let us look to the word of God and in it find refuge from the 'Wherefore?' We ought to know his word, but should not inquire into his will, which is often hidden. That would be to measure wind and fire in our balance scales.[1]

The attitude of the one who prays is one of waiting. The petitioner does not need to attach a "name" to God's help. We do not pray for a specific answer nor even a discernible one. "It is not a bad sign," Luther states, "but a very good one, if things seem to turn out contrary to our requests. Just as it is not a good sign if everything turns out favorable for our requests." [2] Isolating an answer for every petition—to see God's will—is another simple deduction, easy answer, and attempt to prove something starting from the visible.

Somewhat arrogantly, we even try to pass from our own *works* to the holy God. We believe that our achievements and experiences prove God's presence in our lives. We reduce the holiness of God to "sweet feelings," an extravagant effort of religious

22

note, or a mystical event. The reduction of reductions—what counts is being sincere regardless of what you believe. Simple. Easy answer. "Show me thy glory!" So we attribute a flamboyant feeling as appropriate to the presence of God; we construe an uplifting experience as the signal of God's intervention. Appealing to high joy and deep experience, we prove God's existence, so we think. (This might be labeled the "born again" proof.)

But God does not show us his face, just the hinderparts of his being. We cannot see his face and live. All attempts to begin with ourselves and ascend to the invisible, incomprehensible God constitute a deceptive practice. We put the *initiative* in our own hands and eyes, while forgetting that the mind is a "school of lies" and our will an "engine of treachery." We endow causes and forces favorable to us with "goodness"—proof for the glory of God. We select the beautiful and the powerful as signals of God's presence.

Perhaps one of the most glaring examples of this theology of glory is the Moral Majority. Anyone who disagrees with them is both mistaken and malevolent. God is on their side; he even permits them to make the decisions about what is and is not moral. See nice Dick and Jane go to Sunday school. See naughty Nellie and wicked Willie listening to that awful music. They know what is evil. The only trouble is we may know it differently. The Moral Majority has seen God face-to-face and now is ready to face off with the world, demanding that its own certainties become everyone else's.

Actually we have had plenty of Moral Majorities ready to joust with an uneasy universe and to cast the first stone. The Moral Majority in Switzerland burned the reformer John Hus. The Moral Majority in Israel beheaded John the Baptist and in Rome crucified the disciple Peter. The Moral Majority in Salem, Massachusetts drowned witches. In France the Moral Majority burned Joan of Arc. In Germany a Moral Majority exterminated millions of Jews. Need we continue?

The little, near face

God is not to be proven or deduced, but rather believed. Luther said reason is "the devil's bride," easily entranced by whatever can be seen and demonstrated. He called security "the devil's substitute for faith," for the secure person washes his hands of doubt and fills his heart with certainty. But God can only be seen from behind—"God wears a mask, as at Mardi Gras." In all his majesty and power, we can neither see nor know God. God is not naked. He is clothed in his promise. He is hidden in sufferings, his Son's and ours. The only glorious glimpse we get is "the little, near face of Jesus Christ." If we could find God through beauty, power, human achievement, sweet feelings, or a pinpointing of his will, we would simply find, Luther contends, a "vagabond" God. God is identifiable. He promises to be present in his word and sacraments—being gracious to whom he will be gracious and showing mercy to whom he will show mercy.

God clothes his power in the weakness of suffering and cross, in the vulnerability of love. So Luther blurts out—"God in diapers, God at the breast of Mary, God at the carpenter's bench, God on a cross? Who would look to find him there?" [3] God reveals Himself to us as he chooses, strange as it may appear to us. The majesty of God's love is hidden, where from our vantage point all is lost and dark. "God does not want the world to know," says Luther, "when He sleeps with His Bride." [4] It is not our business to know God's business. But we are invited by the Spirit to trust the love of God revealed to us in the suffering and death of Jesus Christ.

The cross marks the chosen spot. There Christ endures physical pain; he suffers loneliness and abandonment. Trial and temptation assault him. The silence and absence of God haunt him. All the anguish of humanity swells in the crest of his passion. "No one has ever seen God," writes the apostle John, "the only Son, who is in the bosom of the Father, he has made him known"

[John 1:14]. But, then, it is still a backside view—cross and suffering. We believe God is for us but not because of his mighty creative power or his eye for design or some handy proof. He is for us precisely where everything, either seemingly or apparently, denies him. Indeed the only son has made God known in the strangest way, where it is hardly possible to "see" him.

Hence, Hans Küng writes:

Even before his death on the cross, Jesus was aware of all the evil in the world, all the injustice, wickedness, cruelty, all the suffering, all the pain, all the grief. But, in the face of all the evil, Jesus did not give any philosophical or theological justification of God, any theodicy. His answer has a practical orientation; it points to God as Father: God as the Father who in his active providence and solicitude looks after every sparrow and every hair, who knows our needs before we ask him, makes our worries seem superfluous; God as the Father who knows about everything in this far from perfect world and without whom nothing happens, whom man can absolutely trust and on whom he can completely rely even in suffering, injustice, sin and death.[5]

The cross points to the Father. It alone reveals the depth of the Father's graciousness. We can trust the Father to find his way to us, even as he found his way into the world, through the only son, strange as cross and suffering may be. He finds us!

Five times I have received at the hands of the Jews the forty lashes less one. Three times I have been beaten with rods; once I was stoned. Three times I have been shipwrecked; a night and a day I have been adrift at sea; on frequent journeys, in danger from rivers, danger from robbers, danger from my own people, danger from Gentiles, danger in the city, danger in the wilderness, danger at sea, danger from false brethren; in toil and hardship, through many a sleepless night, in hunger and thirst, often without food, in cold and exposure. And, apart from other things, there is the daily pressure upon me of my anxiety for all the churches. Who is weak, and I am not weak? Who is made to fall, and I am not indignant? If I must boast, I will boast of the things that show my weakness. . . .

And to keep me from being too elated by the abundance of revelations, a thorn was given me in the flesh, a messenger of Satan, to harass me, to keep me from being too elated. Three times I besought the Lord about this, that it should leave me; but he said to me, "My grace is sufficient for you, for my power is made perfect in weakness." I will all the more gladly boast of my weaknesses, that the power of Christ may rest upon me. For the sake of Christ, then, I am content with weaknesses, insults, hardships, persecutions, and calamities; for when I am weak, then I am strong.

2 CORINTHIANS 11:24-30; 12:7-10

GOD'S STRENGTH IN WEAKNESS

Boasting of weakness

We fear our weaknesses. Maybe we never outgrow the early feelings of being a child—small, inferior, helpless. Even when we grow in stature and maturity, "parent" figures hover over us—the bill collector, the boss, the principal, the pressures of big brother institutions. Shades of Adam—we feel ashamed, appear redfaced, and recognize our naked creatureliness. And we still drape fig leaves over our weak spots: smiling when we feel angry, gushing with compliments but actually feeling disappointment in the other person, acting as if we are vitally pleased in someone's company while in reality we are bored to death. Who can risk letting another know those real feelings, unattractive as they are? Furthermore, we hide behind Adam's bush: our oak-like rationalizations to protect our own skin, our womb-like posture to tuck ourselves inside the power of someone stronger than us. What stubborn stoicism we project in order to cover up our weaknesses!

"Character armor," says the psychiatrist. "Self-righteousness," chimes in the theologian. "Hard-nosed," offers the friend. The teenager blasts: "Phoney!" Regardless of what we may call it, our weaknesses are not for public appearance.

What a complete surprise, to hear the apostle Paul say, "If I must boast, I will boast of the things that show my weakness." What right-minded person boasts in sufferings rather than successes? Listen to Paul's resume—"Five times I have received at the hands of the Jews the forty lashes less one. Three times I have been beaten with rods; once I was stoned. Three times I have been shipwrecked; a night and a day I have been adrift at sea; on frequent journeys, in danger from rivers, danger from robbers, danger from my own people, danger from Gentiles, danger in the city, danger in the wilderness, danger at sea, danger from false brethren; in toil and hardship, through many a sleepless night, in hunger and thirst, often without food, in cold and exposure." Then he goes on to say, "who is weak, and I am not weak?" What is this? Self-pity? Sour grapes? An angry soul? A melancholic hangover? Tearful crying over the spilt milk of life? Just another series of whimperings from a chronic grouch? An outpouring of grief? A bit of public therapy?

Possibly some griping and gloominess loom in the heart of Paul. But we are not about to subject him to clinical evaluation. In fact, the context never indicates any self-hatred, personal loathing, or self-centered pity on Paul's part. We do not hear Paul say that he is horrible, absolutely wretched, a psychic basket case, a milksop, a pushover, a disheartened cripple. Neither can we find in the context an equation between his weakness and sinfulness. We do not hear him saying, "I am a miserable sinner, weighted by my guilt and moral disgust."

If the nature of Paul's weakness is neither psychological nor spiritual, what is it? Paul describes his weakness in relation to others, specifically some opponents who infiltrated the church in Corinth. Evidently these fast-talking philosophers came to denounce Paul's authority and preaching. Like the great Greek sophists of the time—philosophers, debaters, think-tankers—the false apostles tried to win their ideas over by presenting themselves as successful and highly qualified individuals. Translated into modern terms, we would imagine the sophists to be well-credentialed, often-published, and much-publicized spokespersons.

This is not the case with Paul. He takes the position of a sage, who did not rely on his own eloquence, popularity, or colorful success. Rather, the sage contended that his convictions stood tall and true precisely because he had endured trials and troubles. His ideas withstood tribulation; they remained intact despite adversity. Instead of displaying distinguished credits, like his adversaries, Paul stood on his troubles. Paul's message was not authentic because a spotlight rested on it. Out of the crucible of fire, his convictions were tested and formed.

Liabilities as assets

Paul's opponents agreed that the apostles' ideas were "weighty and strong." But they attacked his sickly, bodily presence and speaking ability. Paul's knowledge was noteworthy, but his appearance attracted no second glances and his speech was totally unimpressive. As far as intellect was concerned, he was a "winner," but as for face and voice, he was a real "loser." Nonetheless Paul built on his pain, not his publicity, admitting that to all *appearances* he carried little weight.

Paul admitted to having had visions and revelations just like other philosophers. But what audacity! He could not even remember if he had been caught up into the third heaven in or out of his body. We would expect a public voice to speak with greater self-assurance. But Paul risked speaking with reservation and hesitation, endangering the very authority of his message because of it.

To add injury to insult, Paul's weakness encompassed not merely being hit by the ugly stick, having ordinary speaking skills, or uttering tentative pronouncements, but also bearing a thorn in his flesh—some kind of illness or handicap. With what could he commend himself to his hearers? No tall Texan stature, no commanding voice, no toothpaste ad smile, no wavy hair, dark complexion good looks, no charisma or charm, no glamor-boy image, not even an adequate medical report.

To the Corinthians, Paul was saying that the issue is not the messenger but the message. What counts is not the person who commends himself as either acceptable or honorable, but the person whom the Lord commends. The false apostles who discredited Paul played one of the oldest games in the world. In comparison to them, Paul ran a poor second. Of course, you can score a point for Paul because his thinking was "weighty and strong." When you look at other features, though, he registers numerous negatives. But Paul himself found a flaw in their argument. They compared themselves with one another; they themselves established the criteria for judging the relative ability of a true philosopher. Hence their boasting was self-congratulation. They had set the rules for the game.

Paul proceeds to yet another daring word. "If you want me to boast," he says, "I'll boast of my weaknesses." In effect, Paul is saying that if it is nothing but a boasting campaign, he has something to boast in too—his weakness. Paul has no fiery desire for comparative boasting. But he has a point at which he can boast—his weakness. "My authenticity," Paul claims, "is nothing more than my obvious weaknesses."

Like the crucified Christ

Paul refuses to boast in his well-known knowledge. He will take his chances on what others think according to this principle alone: what they see in him or hear from him. Advertising gimmicks are of no profit. Paul is willing to discount the criteria of fortune and fame, celebrity status, and flourishing enterprises.

How utterly difficult it is for us to understand the man, for even today we gather like flies around the imposing figure, the V.I.P., the luminary. We simply cannot overlook all the stagings, affects, and achievements of well-publicized thinkers and speakers. We make the facile connection between someone's success and truthfulness. We are multipliers and quantifiers. We become aroused by the glory and fame of dignitaries, even in the life of the Christian church. Drawing the conclusion that success spells God's special blessing, we thrust ourselves at the feet and altars of the preaching stars, the organizational whiz kids, and the electronic evangelists.

But Paul envisions his weakness as being close to the very weakness of Christ. Earlier in the letter, he writes, "But we have this treasure in earthen vessels, to show that the transcendent power belongs to God and not to us. We are afflicted in every way, but not crushed; perplexed, but not driven to despair; persecuted, but not forsaken; struck down, but not destroyed; always carrying in the body the death of Jesus, so that the life of Jesus may also be manifested in our bodies" [2 Cor. 4:7-10]. Paul identifies his weakness with Christ's. Paul's bodily weaknesses manifest the life of Jesus. Paul wants nothing but Christ crucified —no fluff, no extras, no icing. Precisely in weakness God's grace is powerful—"for when I am weak, then I am strong." Paul's weakness makes him one with the Lord, "for he was crucified in weakness" [2 Cor. 13:4].

The weakness gospel

How can we relate this to our own experience? Attracted to outward, external appearances, we can overlook the message because of the earthen vessel in which it is contained. It is not what we expect. Perhaps the messenger is frail, ordinary, or unknown. What could we ever learn from such a person? But Herman G. Stuempfle Jr. remarks:

God does not require superior material or promising circumstances to accomplish his purposes. I heard in a new way the meaning of Isaiah's familiar words, 'We are the clay, and thou art the potter' (64:8). God is able to take up the most ordinary and unimpressive material and shape it to his design. As Nikos Kazantzakis once put it, if God is indeed a potter then it must follow that 'he works with mud!' [1]

And if God can work with creatures formed from mud, he can certainly work in muddy situations—weaknesses, insults, hardships, persecutions, and calamities. In updating Paul's personal list, we would claim that God can work in loneliness, cancer, when feelings of rejection swell inside of us, when death leaves us with bitter sorrow, and when fame is absent.

How hard it is to resist the appeal of things that are seen! We have second thoughts about this "weakness gospel." When things and people dazzle and radiate energy, we are instinctively drawn to attention. When life is wine and roses, we quite naturally assume God's presence, for he is good and loving. We boast in our fame, honors, and glory. But at the same time, we are the ones who have decided where the line of boasting begins—our perceptions, our desires, our creations. Paul's vision is different. God is a God who works through contraries. He can work through weakness. Even more, the grace of God is perfect in our weakness, at the time and point when to all appearances God is hidden. Who could know it any better than Paul? He has written in this same letter to the Corinthians that "our life is a matter of faith, not sight" [2 Cor. 5:7]. But this phrase had not been etched for him in the heavens or carved on a stone he stumbled over during his journeys. He squirmed and wiggled over his infirmity. Three times by prayer he asked for the removal of the pain that cut into his wholeness. He had a just fear of the weakness that others used against him in their attempt to cancel his "weighty and strong" thoughts, and that bedeviled his own freedom and selfhood. Weighted and grounded, he knew firsthand that sight could never carry him beyond the affliction. He could theorize or rationalize; he could compensate or complain. He could travel to a shrine or engage a "shrink." But nothing could make it as plain as pie. Paul could "see" affliction as a gift only through faith. God's *alien* work leads to his *proper* work, Luther would say centuries later. Affliction exists not for mere teaching value, as we might imply when we say, "learning from mistakes" or "trial and error." Affliction can issue in curses and cries for revenge. Instead of turning the sufferer to prayers and praise, the weakness throws a person inward, upon the self. Paul could have become all thorn in the flesh just as our children become all poison ivy, obsessed with itching.

Our weakness is for cleansing, for grace, and for faith to assert itself. To sight, however, it is absurd. The cross of the crucified Christ extricates us from nothing in life. But it announces a strength that is complete in weakness, a love steadfast in the most remote island of discontent, a forgiveness far deeper than an early parole, a power that will not exploit our weakness, but in it and from it will bring a gift, that is, trust in the grace of God. Luther compared our weak humanity to the printer's block with letters set backward. In this life we read affliction backward, from sight, as nonsense. We need patience until the time comes when we read the afflictions properly, as only God knows for what purpose they serve.

Frederick Buechner lays bare the reality of the cross and weakness:

... God shows us a man who gave his life away to the extent of dying a national disgrace without a penny in the bank or a friend to his name. In terms of men's wisdom, he was a Perfect Fool, and anybody who thinks he can follow him without making something like the same kind of a fool of himself is laboring under not a cross but a delusion.[2]

Strength in weakness—it is no ideal solution, no self-evident truth. And yet, the cross points to the evil, the affliction, or whatever the weakness, and, regardless of its severity or absurdity and our fearfulness of it, invites us to believe that God can turn everything to good—enmity to reconciliation, weakness to strength, and troubles to triumph.

And Mary said, "My soul magnifies the Lord, and my spirit rejoices in God my Savior, for he has regarded the low estate of his handmaiden. For behold, henceforth all generations will call me blessed; for he who is mighty has done great things for me, and holy is his name. And his mercy is on those who fear him from generation to generation. He has shown strength with his arm, he has scattered the proud in the imagination of their hearts, he has put down the mighty from their thrones, and exalted those of low degree; he has filled the hungry with good things, and the rich he has sent empty away. He has helped his servant Israel, in remembrance of his mercy, as he spoke to our fathers, to Abraham and to his posterity for ever."

LUKE 1:46-55

IN THE EYES OF
THE DIVINE BEHOLDER

God's story

Mother Goose's Mary had a little lamb. God's Mary did not
have much more. Perhaps she did not have so much as a lamb.
Luther describes her as being of "low estate and nothingness,"
who "came of poor, despised, and lowly parents," and was nothing more than "a poor and plain citizen's daughter, whom none
looked up to or esteemed." [1] But God *regarded* her. And that is
a whole new story. Lamb or no lamb, Mary was to bear in her
womb the "lamb of God" who would take away the sins of the
world. Indeed God chooses what is low and despised in the
world to bring to nothing things that are. In the eyes of the
Divine Beholder, Mary is regarded; that is, she is favored and
graced despite her father's poverty line salary, her own early
adolescence, and her unpretentious genealogy. We are about to
hear a story of how God sees things—a flesh-and-earth account
of God choosing that which is weak, foolish, and humble to accomplish his gracious purposes.

But this is no rags to riches, log cabin to White House, chore
girl to Cinderella tale. It is, rather, a story line from angels to
manger, and from manger to Egypt, and from Egypt to Nazareth,

and from Nazareth to Cana, and from the wedding wine of Cana to the "I thirst" of cross and Calvary. In fact, it is much less a story of Mary and her low estate and far more a story of God who has the eyes to see even the low ones and *regard* them. "God's work and his eyes are in the depths, but man's only in the heights" (Luther).[2]

The low ones and the depths

The Divine Beholder baffles us. He sees the depths. Precisely. That's precisely what Luther drives at when he speaks of God appearing "under the opposite form," working in ways that "are always unattractive," and revealing himself "only in suffering and the cross." We *assume* that God works in the high and lofty, among the religious elite, with those who have clout and charm. And we *expect* that a Divine Beholder, full of power and glory, would be impressed with earthly counterparts sharing these qualities. But this is *eros:* like attracted to like. God is a God of *agape,* overcoming differences and distortions, the ugly and the outsider, the gaps and the cleavages. *Eros* seeks correspondence; *agape* involves contradiction. *Eros* centers on that which is beautiful, powerful, and similar. But *agape* is creative, embracing what is unusual, unseemly, and unknown. It is a suffering love for neglected, abandoned, and deceived human beings. In a striking note, Kisoh Kitamori states in *The Theology of The Pain of God* that God embraces those "who should not be embraced."

Mary is not the first lowly one reported as God's choice. The children of Israel are chosen as the least of all the peoples of the earth, with no *apparent* recommendation for their being chosen. And yet the primary reason for the selection may have been that they lacked credentials. All qualifications aside, the children of Israel would have no cause for glorifying themselves instead of Yahweh. Moses, though touted a hero, was nothing more than a son of slaves, in need of speech therapy, and even a murderer. David's plain and ordinary status is known—a shepherd boy

36

Then, too, note the Chronicler's description of Saul in 1 Samuel 9, reporting Saul as coming "from the least of the tribes of Israel" and "from the humblest of all the families of the tribe of Benjamin."

Moreover, notice how *younger* sons fare in the Scriptures. Though it was normal to favor the oldest son and the legitimate heir, Jacob's intrigue netted him his brother's birthright, and Jacob himself favored his younger sons, Joseph and Benjamin. Abel, the younger brother, had his offering accepted by God, to the complete anger of Cain the elder. This break with tradition is evident too with David and Solomon. Furthermore, the *helpless* are a special concern to the writer of Deuteronomy. They include the slave (15:15), the sojourner or stranger (10:18-19), the orphan, and the widow (24:17-18, 19-22).

In the New Testament more lowly ones appear: shepherds are ushered to the crib, a lost sheep is the object of a search party, a child serves as the principle example of the citizen of the kingdom of God. Like the children of Israel, the little band of people comprising the emerging church are said not to have been wise according to worldly standards, not many of noble birth, not many powerful. Speaking of sons, everyone is aware of how the elder brother in Jesus' parable fell flat on his religious nose while the younger one comes to new life through his father's love.

When the writers of the New Testament sought an appropriate metaphor for Jesus, they reached into the fifty-third chapter of Isaiah and the suffering servant poems: "no form or comeliness that we should look at him, and no beauty that we should desire him. . . . a man of sorrows . . . and as one from whom men hide their faces, he was despised, and we esteemed him not" [vv. 2-3]. Whether or not we interpret this to mean that he was either physically ugly or relatively obscure misses the point. He was *counted* among the lowly ones. In turn, he counts the lowly ones as "blessed"—the poor in spirit, the meek, the needy. This unexpected turn of affairs caused Luther to say, "all His works are such that out of that which is nothing, worthless, despised, wretched, and dead, He makes that which is something, precious, honorable, blessed, and living." [3]

A blow to pity

But Friedrich Nietzsche uses this very argument to raise slashing objections to Christianity. He considers the Christian conception of God—that is, God of the sick, God as spirit, God as "spider"—to be a "corrupt conception" of God.

Nietzsche hammers harder and scorns Christianity for siding "with all that is weak and base, with all failures" and for making "an ideal of whatever contradicts the instinct of the strong to preserve itself." He calls Jesus "that holy anarchist" who scours the bottom of the barrel and gathers up the outcast and the condemned. All the nobodies, the less valuable, the bruised and the betrayed, the miserable lot, the inferior, the afflicted are "on top all at once." Repulsed, Nietzsche strikes at *pity*. It is nothing but an instrument to heap weakness upon weakness. To Nietzsche, the "crouch to the cross" is the loss of "morning valor"—whatever is healthy, robust, vital, and strong. Jesus who dies the death of a slave—a cross—is the antithesis to strength and height. Nietzsche rejects the idea of a God who embraces people at the bottom, souls crushed under anguish, and victims of invisibility.

We pay a subtle homage to this Nietzschean disgust. We have our own practice of "shunning," from the refugee to the young person who thinks he or she is worthless. And we engage in a not-so-subtle worship of the vigorous and mighty; we distort the importance of the beautiful people, the rich and powerful, the superstar and celebrity, even the self-assertive and the intimidator. Our eyes are in the height.

Where God begins

But God *begins* where from our perspective everything is lost and forgotten. He regards the low ones, such as Mary. Her "low estate" indicates humility, poverty, barrenness, and humiliation. In the Old Testament it is a description of the persecuted and oppressed. The "poor ones" in Jewish society encompass more than those who are physically deprived. Among their number are the sick, the downtrodden, and the afflicted—anyone who could not rely on their own strength but must trust in the bare mercy of God. Their opposites are the arrogant and self-sufficient who obviously display no need of God or his mercy. Writing in his commentary on the Magnificat, Luther says:

> Humility, therefore, is nothing else than a disregarded, despised, and lowly estate, such as that of men who are poor, sick, hungry, thirsty, in prison, suffering, and dying. Such was Job in his afflictions, David when he was thrust out of his kingdom, and Christ as well as all Christians, in their distresses. Those are the depths of which we said above that God's eyes look only into them, but men's only to the heights, namely, to that which is splendid and glorious and makes a brave show.[4]

For Luther no one can know God apart from his regard for the lowly. Again, this is why the subject of the story is not Mary, but God. He *regards* her. God is the benedictor. His eyes focus on Mary, graciously and mercifully, in spite of all her lowliness. God makes his face to shine upon her and is gracious unto her; God lifts up his countenance upon her and grants her peace. In Mary's own words: "He has helped his servant Israel, in remembrance of his mercy. . . ." God's abundant grace embraces and blesses this unregarded creature—nothing but "amazing."

False spirits

So when Luther turns his attention to "false spirits that cannot sing the Magnificat aright," he condemns two types of glory-seekers.[5] First, the people who look only to the heights for a blessing, one, at that, which carries a reward or a result. Unless God does well to us, we are "unable to love and praise the bare, unfelt goodness that is hidden in God." We experience tragedy

39

and refuse to lay aside the excruciating question, "why did this happen to me?" Angry, we hold the pain *against* God. Sadly, we linger in our disappointment and become thin of soul. According to Luther, we "sing only when it fares well" and "as soon as it fares ill, we stop our singing and no longer esteem God highly." [6] We have looked up and striven for what is above only to discover our empty hands and unanswered lips. God hides his face and the radiancy of his goodness, leaving us barren and miserable. We find ourselves without love, praise, and thankfulness for his goodness. Luther says this is delighting in salvation rather than a Savior, in the gift instead of the giver, in the creature in place of the Creator.

More dangerous yet are the other kind who "are on the opposite side." The "regard" is self-endowed. Appropriating the gifts of God as their own, they set themselves above others. They "fall upon" the good things apart from any acknowledgement of God's goodness alone. While the former fall upon the goodness of God for safety, playing low profile until the threat passes by, the second group seizes the gifts as rights and powers. Postured or feigned lowliness is wretched enough. But brazen souls in the next category cannot even conceive of lowliness. They see the heights, never once glancing at the source of all their benefits.

Daniel Boorstin, writing in *Democracy and Its Discontents,* muses: "There is an obvious cure for failure—and that is success. But what is the cure for success?" What cures us from the tyranny of playing "king of the mountain"? What happens when we are immune to being taken down a peg or two? In the heights we are "high-blown, puffed-up, stuck-up, stiff-necked." Success bears its own curses and banes. It crosses out in bold marks the whole idea of grace, receiving, and dependency. Success in itself is neither good nor bad. It is the nature of success, however, to be deceptive. No cures are necessary. All angles are covered in safety and back-up systems. Success denies contingency, mortality, and community. We become do-it-ourselves gods when we fall upon the gifts of God as our own. And if we are constantly looking down on others from our lofty perch, we are not able to look up at God or around for our neighbor.

We forget that Narcissus, who fell in love with his reflection, was being *punished* by the gods for his vanity. In a sense, succcess can be its own punishment, especially if it is illusory, leading us down the primrose path of bloated importance. Not surprisingly, then, Luther addresses his treatise on the Magnificat "To his Serene Highness, Prince John Frederick, Duke of Saxony," saying that since the great and mighty "need not fear men" of all people they "should fear God more than others do." The Magnificat is far more than a lyrical hymn for the lowly. It is a warning cry to the self-encased glorifiers: God *regards*. And being no respecter of persons, he comes and invites, promises and offers, stirs up and confers his gracious love for Christ's sake, laying the mighty low and making the low great—on equal footing before a cross.

Jeremiah said, "The word of the Lord came to me: Behold, Hanamel the son of Shallum your uncle will come to you and say, 'Buy my field which is at Anathoth, for the right of redemption by purchase is yours.' Then Hanamel my cousin came to me in the court of the guard, in accordance with the word of the Lord, and said to me, 'Buy my field which is at Anathoth in the land of Benjamin, for the right of possession and redemption is yours; buy it for yourself.' Then I knew that this was the word of the Lord.

"And I bought the field at Anathoth from Hanamel my cousin, and weighed out the money to him, seventeen shekels of silver. I signed the deed, sealed it, got witnesses, and weighed the money on scales. Then I took the sealed deed of purchase, containing the terms and conditions, and the open copy; and I gave the deed of purchase to Baruch the son of Neriah son of Mahseiah, in the presence of Hanamel my cousin, in the presence of the witnesses who signed the deed of purchase, and in the presence of all the Jews who were sitting in the court of the guard. I charged Baruch in their presence, saying, 'Thus says the Lord of Hosts, the God of Israel: Take these deeds, both this sealed deed of purchase and this open deed, and put them in an earthenware vessel, that they may last for a long time. For thus says the Lord of hosts, the God of Israel: Houses and fields and vineyards shall again be bought in this land.' "

JEREMIAH 32:6-15

GOD'S FUTURE IS TODAY

Foolish hope

Hope begins in its own absence. For us, hope is a strength when the situation is hopeless. Hope starts with an empty cup; it begins at a dead end or in the wilderness.

Hope is not high optimism based on previous success. There is undoubtedly a confidence born from the past. Success breeds success. But it is not necessarily hope. Optimists carry the odds in their back pocket. They build on the past record. The hopeful build in the opposite direction: expectation, anticipation, the future. Optimists run full steam ahead *because of* what they have or know. But the hopeful reach for what is ahead *in spite of* a mixed or depleted bag of positive experiences. They rely on dreams, promises, and visions.

Hope is always exaggeration. It is hyperbole. In time and space, hope always promises more than it delivers. We never shed the shell of our limitations. Hope does not, therefore, rest on the belief that "something better" is in the works. Hope gives energy to courage and imagination. It thrives on what is possible and what is promising. But actual improvement may not come. Hope is a struggle against the odds, even against deteriorating

43

circumstances. Someone has defined hope as faith written in the future tense, another as faith on tiptoes. Hope is the great "nevertheless" spoken by Job, for instance, in a miserable circumstance —"Behold, he will slay me . . . yet I will defend my ways to his face" [13:15].

In the vignette of Jeremiah's purchase of a piece of land, we confront the bold hope of the prophet. At face value it is a terrible real estate investment. It is, at least from a business point of view, a facetious venture. The Babylonians are on the doorsteps to seize the beleaguered city. The smell of carnage infiltrates the air. Defeat with a capital "D" is spelled out in the mind of the most determined optimist. For the moment, the "healthy-minded," despite their ingrained buoyancy, must stand beside the "sick-minded" in their view of the tragic. Jeremiah himself sits imprisoned for having prophesied what was taking place. King Zedekiah, having more than enough problems with military defense, cannot tolerate a gloomy prophet. Call it what you may— panic or pandemonium, a crisis or a crazy, mixed-up affair—buying a plot of land already in the fingertips of the enemy is absurd. But Jeremiah follows the instructions of "the word of the Lord." A specified price is wagered, the money is weighed, the deed is signed in the presence of the necessary witnesses, the witnesses in turn sign their names, and the documents are stored in the earthenware safety deposit box "that they may last for a long time." What profit or benefit would Jeremiah ever receive? In essence, Jeremiah is investing in certificates of deposit non-redeemable for decades, probably centuries. Jeremiah's hope is not only inflated but also ridiculous.

Nothing too hard

What is the connection between the apparent "bad deal" of Jeremiah and the cross of Jesus? The apostle Paul presents a startling point, saying, "While we were still weak, at the right time Christ died for the ungodly. Why, one will hardly die for a righteous man—though perhaps for a good man one will dare even to die. But God shows his love for us in that while we were yet sinners Christ died for us" [Rom. 5:6-8]. Helpless to cash in for gain, Jeremiah nonetheless buys the land at Anathoth, according to both the command of the Lord, "Buy my field," and his promise, "Houses and fields and vineyards shall again be bought in this land." We, too, helpless to cash in our spiritual checks, stand before God's command and promise. From the viewpoint of profit, God gains little in his reconciling work, the death of Christ. Yet "God shows his love," and gains those who are "still weak" and "yet sinners" and "enemies." Consequently we can "rejoice in our hope of sharing the glory of God" [Rom. 5:2]. That glory is not fully ours, just as the promise of a building boom and bumper crop to Jeremiah was not fully his. But "hope does not disappoint us." For Jeremiah the reason is given in his confession: "Nothing is too hard for thee, who showest steadfast love to thousands" [32:17-18]. And likewise for Paul, the reason is the same, "because God's love has been poured into our hearts through the Holy Spirit which has been given to us" [5:5].

Hope begins in its own absence, a city besieged and a Christ crucified. Exactly when everything looks less than promising, the promise is already germinating—like a seed in the darkness of the soil. So the theology of the cross constantly reminds us that God wills to be known in the dark places, comes to the place where it is hard to find him, and works in the trouble spots. Alone, we cannot grasp this, but Jeremiah's purchase of land and Jesus' redemption of sinners points us in this direction. God hides his majesty and power behind a *veil*. Through a glass or mirror, from behind and in weakness, in a hopeless situation, we still come to know and trust the sufficiency of God's gracious love. For God clothes his power in the love and suffering of Christ and in our own suffering as well. And his power is not primarily a resource to retrieve us from pain and helplessness, defeat and failure. It is strength, not solution—"they who wait for the Lord shall renew their strength, they shall mount up with wings like eagles, they shall run and not be weary, they shall walk and not faint" (Isa. 40:31). Hope is the strength to live through the odds and adversities. It is based on promise. Hence, Jeremiah purchased a slice of "the promised land" at Anathoth, even though encumbered with the imminent Babylonian lien. And God invests himself in history and on a cross—in spite of debts and charges and sins against us. To Jeremiah, there came the promises of restored fortunes; to us, there comes the promise that if anyone is in Christ, there is a new creation.

The promise holds

Although hope may exceed reality, without it we grope and, not finding, we complain. Four or five steps into complaining, we set on the territory of weariness and approach a city without gates called Despair. Having centuries of hindsight, we can make sense of the sale at Anathoth. In our own lives, though, we have no hindsight to justify our hopes. We plod and run; we make resolve and focus our eyes ahead. Anticipation lies within the realm of the pleasure principle. But the dog-eared reality principle has not gone to sleep. Hopes rock back and forth. If anything, our hindsight begins to emerge, only now questioning why we ever put our money on the land, our dreams on the future, or our lives on the promises of God. "Anathoth" is spoken with derision and as a curse.

Maybe Joseph Sittler's words make sense of the experience of putting the promise before the what was and the what is (what we call "time-honored" realities).

". . . one begins to see that the judgment of God is at work in the failure of our successes, in the negative results that come in for what we believe to be completely positive actions. When the things in which we have rested our hope turn out to be unable to deliver the goods which we had hoped for, this is grace by way of judgment; it's education by way of disappointment and illumination by way of darkness. As in the Old Testament, God led them home by way of the wilderness. That's not the most comfortable way to go home, but it may be the only way in some periods.

Take Psalm 23—who would think you would find anything new there? I was sitting in chapel and I heard the reader say: "Even though I walk through the valley of the shadow of death, I will fear no evil; . . ." Look at that phrase. You walk through the valley of the shadow of death—not just the valley of death. The valley of death is the moment you die, but all your life you walk through a valley over which the shadow of death moves. You move toward death. That's not just rhetoric. "Walk through the valley of the shadow" says that we live toward non-living; we move toward non-being. We move every day toward the moment when we shall not move at all. The whole of life is a valley under the shadow of death and the only way to overcome it is to know that." [1]

Here, having "no lasting city," we must pass through wilderness and valley. I must die. The question is, How shall I live? Jeremiah's purchase of land provides a hint. I shall live by a promise. For if Jeremiah had lived by common sense and plain sight, he would have left his money in the bank. A promise frees us from observing and understanding in one way only. Single visions affirm only a part of life. They concentrate on one corner of reality. The rest of reality is repressed and lies dormant, hidden, and obscure. But wilderness and valleys engender a strange truth, noted by Luther: "To be born anew, one must consequently first die and then be raised up with the Son of Man. To die, I say, means to feel death at hand." [2] Hope dwells in the emptiness. And while it promises more than it delivers in the moment, it nevertheless delivers. Isaiah, with the-poet's touch, affirms such hope: "Arise, shine; for your light has come, and the glory of the Lord has risen upon you. For behold, darkness shall cover the earth, and thick darkness the peoples; but the Lord will arise upon you, and his glory will be seen upon you" [Isa. 60:1-2]. God is at work opening up his glory by sending a little bewilderment into our lives. Hope is seeing with a wide lens. Our field of vision is not narrowed to a single point of view, to a few sensations, to the moment, to a solitary experience, to an isolated piece of security. Hope opens us to a full range of life: we can hear as well as see, we can smell as well as touch, we can wonder as well as pinpoint. It is this chaos of Jerusalem crumbling, this very disintegration, that can be a time for grace. Everything we have known and have trusted may fall apart with the onslaught of so great a force. Suddenly we recognize a knowledge laid aside: our lives are like an experiment whose ultimate outcome we are not about to know. Our vision is partial, and yet at the same time it is fuller. We don't "see" the full-blown picture, but we trust that God sees everything. We need to see nothing. We live between the times but at all times the promise holds. Grace is hidden, to be sure, even hidden under its opposite. And grace, like the hope it arouses in hopeless times, begins its mighty work in its apparent absence.

We can find similarity between Jeremiah's action at Anathoth and the tale of a man plucking strawberries while wedged between two hungry tigers. Pursued by tiger A, he was chased over a cliff and hung precariously on a vine dangling from the side of the hill. Glancing below, he saw menacing tiger B. Above his hands two mice gnawed steadily on the vine. His eyes discovered a clump of wild strawberries. With one hand free he picked the fruit, eating and exclaiming, "How delicious!"

Eyes for strawberries! Hope is more than a stubborn holding on or resolutely planning ahead. It is seeing a promise in the most unpromising situation: joy in sorrow, forgiveness in despair, mercy in disaster. Hope is an awareness of tigers and mice and the taste of strawberries. It is to have knowledge of Babylonian swords clattering and smoke rising and yet making a purchase of land for the sake of the promise.

God's future is today. Eternity has entered time, and there is more time than we ever imagined. Vineyards shall again be bought in the land of Anathoth! Yes, even wild, delicious strawberry patches! The promise is as good *today* as it will be tomorrow, even though it looks tarnished in our hands at the

48

moment. The truth of the promise is not its fulfillment, its effects, its evidences, or its blessings. The truth of the promise depends on the power of the promiser.

"For it is God," Paul says, "who has shone in our hearts to give the light of the knowledge of the glory of God in the face of Christ" [2 Cor. 4:6]. He is the sign and the reality that nothing "is too hard for thee who showest steadfast love to thousands. . . ." Hence, we do not have to lie about the darkness of Babylonian assault or Zedekiah's failure. Nor do we need to gloss over the stains and strains of our human experience. Optimism is not the generator of hope. The *ground* of hope lies in the possibility of God's promise, not its necessity. It is grace. God may lead us into the deep night but always with the promise that the day is at hand. So we remain prisoners of hope. And hope begins in its own absence.

We hope. We hope not because it is necessary for good to triumph ultimately. That's human optimism; that's wishful thinking. We hope because God is faithful to his promises—and everything becomes *possible,* today and tomorrow.

Luther reminds us that God accomplished his mightiest act in apparent defeat—the cross. Like the purchase at Anathoth, Jesus' trip to Jerusalem speaks of folly and failure. To perceive "glory" through a real estate rip-off or a suffering man is far beyond us. The implications are frustrating, as William Muehl convincingly argues:

A carrot held just beyond a donkey's nose will often activate the beast to forward movement. But a carrot held so far beyond his nose that there is obviously no chance whatever of his reaching it will soon strike even a jackass as poor judgment for effort! [3]

How can we hope when we choose to lick our wounds in self-pity after the loss of a loved one? How can we believe when we brood, watching a child suffer? How can we rejoice when anger bottles us up because of a random, haphazard accident? At these times promise is a carrot far beyond our noses.

That's the human story, isn't it? Real and messy. Acute and painful. Anathoth and Jerusalem are God's story, just as concrete and confusing as our experience. God is there. He suffers with us. We may covet the carrot, but the best we can *hope* for is the promise that God's future is today—for Christ's sake.

"When the Son of man comes in his glory, and all the angels with him, then he will sit on his glorious throne. Before him will be gathered all the nations, and he will separate them one from another as a shepherd separates the sheep from the goats, and he will place the sheep at his right hand, but the goats at the left. Then the King will say to those at his right hand, 'Come, O blessed of my Father, inherit the kingdom prepared for you from the foundation of the world; for I was hungry and you gave me food, I was thirsty and you gave me drink, I was a stranger and you welcomed me, I was naked and you clothed me, I was sick and you visited me, I was in prison and you came to me.' Then the righteous will answer him, 'Lord, when did we see thee hungry and feed thee, or thirsty and give thee drink? And when did we see thee a stranger and welcome thee, or naked and clothe thee? And when did we see thee sick or in prison and visit thee?' And the King will answer them, 'Truly, I say to you, as you did it to one of the least of these my brethren, you did it to me.' Then he will say to those at his left hand, 'Depart from me, you cursed, into the eternal fire prepared for the devil and his angels; for I was hungry and you gave me no food, I was thirsty and you gave me no drink, I was a stranger and you did not welcome me, naked and you did not clothe me, sick and in prison and you did not visit me.' Then they also will answer, 'Lord, when did we see thee hungry or thirsty or a stranger or naked or sick or in prison, and did not minister to thee?' Then he will answer them, 'Truly, I say to you, as you did it not to one of the least of these, you did it not to me.' And they will go away into eternal punishment, but the righteous into eternal life."

MATTHEW 25:31-46

THE DARKNESS
WHERE GOD IS

Light and darkness

The story surges back and forth. It is darkness to light and back to darkness. From beginning to end the tension mounts. In Genesis we read that "darkness was upon the face of the deep" [1:2], and way back there in Revelation, "night shall be no more" [22:5]. Between the covers are the dark days of Egypt and the lighter times under the rule of King Solomon. God's people linger in the obscurity of Babylon, captive and heart-broken. And then it is the return to their own land with brighter days ahead through Nehemiah's reforms. At night the shepherds receive the angel's announcement of the birth of Christ. In the morning hours tongues of fire ignite a Pentecost celebration hardly repeatable today. From Friday's noon to midday, "there was darkness over the whole land" [Mark 15:33], even as the dying figure on the cross cast his own dark shadow over those beneath him. When Sunday's dawn peeped into the tomb, only the burial linens were visible. Light and darkness are set in a continuous volley—the bright cloud at the Exodus merely to be followed by the drab wilderness, on the heels of the star of Bethlehem comes the black madness of Herod's slaughter of children, and Samaritans recognize "the light of the world" while Pharisees hide in the caves of their tradition.

God comes in light and darkness. Both day and night compose the story of God's work in our lives. Someone has even said that we can see further in the darkness because we have to *probe*. The faculty of awareness expands with the blurring of edges and the melting of outlines, in the absence of landmarks and signposts, through the minimizing of control and the diminishing of sight. Other senses are called to be alert. Prophets and therapists have described the "dark night of the soul," the intrusive and nagging anguish that comes to every one of us: the loss of a friend, a shattered home, the failure of health, wilting stress, thin faith that no longer engenders courage, and random injustices. In the biblical story we recall Jacob's dark night of the soul in his nocturnal struggle at the Jabbok river. Likewise, the prayers of Gethsemane—garden though it be—filled the dark and missed the disciples who had surrendered to their drowsiness.

Beyond the biblical story, we discover the dark night of the soul in many human stories. Writing from a psychological viewpoint, Robert Jay Lifton notes that "renewal . . . is impossible to achieve without forays into danger, destruction, and negativity." Victor Turner, an anthropologist, describes life in the margins, where a person passes from one state to another, in these words—" 'being in a tunnel' . . . sometimes mysterious darkness." Family therapist Salvador Minuchen contends that without crisis there is no transformation. Ernest Becker suggests that growth takes place in the teeth of breakdown. The human story surges back and forth, light to darkness and darkness to light.

In all troubles

We are introspective types, digging in the trenches of our psyche. We concern ourselves with the soul's plight: motives, self-esteem, feelings, and inner states. Without second thought, we can speak of God's "entrance into darkness" and the "fogs and shadows" (using Luther's words) to signify the inscrutability of mystery, intrigue, and depth. In unison with Luther, we can say that the horrible mask which hides God's face cannot be drawn away, rather, we must remain in "exceedingly dark mist" until God shines his light on us.[1] God hides. He works in the unattractive places; he contradicts all appearances. God conceals himself and comes to us in dark moments. Quite easily, we associate God's activity in the depth of our soul or the twilight of our psyche.

But the twenty-fifth chapter of Matthew directs us to another darkness, one less discernible and sometimes more problematic—the *dark night of the body*. I am not making a facile distinction between spirit and matter, or soul and body, as if no connection exists between them. We know they are linked together as suggested by the insights of psychosomatic medicine, wholistic health, spirituality and the mystics, developmental psychology, and a variety of individual experiences. Nonetheless it is tempting and very practical to connect God's gracious care almost exclusively with our inner self-worth at the expense of regard for somatic hunger and thirst. Our own felt needs, whether issuing from fear or loneliness, seem to be the appropriate place for God's love and presence, yet with great neglect of the same for the meals of the imprisoned. Certainly our felt insecurity deserves a mighty God's attention. But the fragility of the stranger hovers in the background, where God someday may be attentive.

The hungry, the thirsty, the naked, the prisoner, the sick, the stranger—they are the ones who experience the dark night of the body. To be sure, we who live in the "psychological society" have difficulty in perceiving the concern and presence of God in the "third world," where the hungry and naked are apt to be. We who have been conditioned to think of the "self" and the "ego" have a blind side to "sharing" and "interdependence" on a wide scale. Let a preacher speak about how God can heal the bruises of the human psyche and observe the listeners perking up their ears. Then let the same speaker refer to the massiveness of hunger and God's presence in the need of the hungry and the same ears lose their tautness.

The "art" of the theology of the cross is to see God in suffering and misery but not only in our own. The cross addresses itself to the world's distresses, including those of the body. Luther writes: "He does not say with this or that difficulty, but simply says, 'all who are heavy laden' . . . he not only refreshes us in the anxiety and assaults of sin, but he will be with us in all other troubles." [2] In Jesus Christ God identified with the hungry, the stranger, the oppressed, the sick, and the imprisoned. And Jesus himself answered the question of his messiahship by identifying himself with the lame who walk and the blind who see. Even today, God identifies with the stranger, the needy, the refugee, the mentally retarded—"the least of these my brethren."

For service

The story begins, "When the Son of man comes in his glory. . . ." The spotlight falls on the lofty appearance of Christ in majesty and power. It is judgment time, a separation of the sheep from the goats. *Invited* to stand at the favored right hand are the "blessed." They are *inheritors* of the kingdom *prepared* for them. Most noteworthy, the sheep at the right hand are there by invitation: "Come, O blessed of my Father." They inherit the kingdom, they do not storm it. They are recipients ("prepared"), not the well-deserving. This is not an awards banquet. The blessed are *not* those who have kept their side of the deal. None are esteemed for their churchgoing or their moral behavior. To the contrary, the blessed are hardly conscious of doing anything. Whatever they did, it was done without calculation, gain, or preoccupation. Premeditation is absent; "when did we. . . .'" they ask in amazement.

Paul Pruyser tells the story of a radio evangelist who attacked the editors of a new translation of the Bible because they had substituted the word "rooms" for "mansions" in the text: "In my Father's house are many rooms" (John 14:2). The preacher considered this to be a shortening of God's promises. If the King James version promised a mansion, why settle for a single room? He was regarding a promise as if it were a business contract, and he was going to cash in the promissory note. That is a confusion of darkness with light. We deserve nothing. A promise is a promise. But we are not to determine its time, its shape, its presence, its fulfillment. Promises are not demand notes, neither are they contractual terms. Promises are freely given and amazingly tendered.

Jesus identifies himself with the needy, but not for the reason of sentimentality: "What a shame!" His identification does not stem from sheer morality: "Let us all be kind!" No trace of expediency enters the discussion, "Help yourself by helping another!" None of the typical American mores are evident, such as the disposition to favor the underdog. If we do anything to or for the least of people, it is for no other reason than the intrinsic good news and saving power of the gospel. God has come to release us from preoccupation with the *self,* its rights and privileges, its morality and sufficiency, its intentions and motives. We are, says Luther, turned in on ourselves. We are in bondage, precisely at the level of *willing.* The good we intend to do, we leave undone. The evil we abhor, we embrace. The power of the gospel of Jesus Christ sets us free from a tyranny—"Every one who commits sin is a slave to sin" [John 8:34]. The cross of the crucified one not only frees us *from* the tyrants of sin, death, and the devil but also *for* feeding the hungry, visiting the sick, and welcoming the stranger. He who has transferred us from the kingdom of darkness into his marvelous light empowers us to become a light to those who sit in the darkness of their bodies.

Comfort reaches out

The twenty-fifth chapter of Matthew culminates a long story of light and darkness. It does not hang in midair; it is not a last minute threat to shape up the work of charity among us. Consider these previous words in Matthew's gospel:

"Blessed are the merciful, for they shall obtain mercy" [5:7].

"He who finds his life will lose it, and he who loses his life for my sake will find it" [10:39].

"And stretching out his hand toward his disciples, he said, 'Here are my mother and my brothers! For whoever does the will of my Father in heaven is my brother, and sister, and mother'" [12:49-50].

"Whoever receives one such child in my name receives me" [18:5].

"So the last will be first, and the first last" [20:16].

"And he said to him, 'You shall love the Lord your God with all your heart, and with all your soul, and with all your mind. This is the great and first commandment. And a second is like it. You shall love your neighbor as yourself" [22:37-39].

"He who is greatest among you shall be your servant; whoever exalts himself will be humbled, and whoever humbles himself will be exalted" [23:11-12].

We cannot see or imagine the presence of Christ in the darkness of physical suffering if we ourselves are closed to the grace of God. Graciousness is born of grace. Love is the action of faith in the direction of the neighbor. "We love because he first loved us," says the apostle John [4:19]; "his compassion is over all that he has made," adds the psalmist [145:9].

Matthew 25 is an invitation to us, not to a theology of glory, but to the theology of the cross. The God who "comforts us in all our affliction" bids us to "comfort those who are in any affliction, with the comfort with which we ourselves are comforted by God" [2 Cor. 1:4]. We who can see the presence of God in the dark night of the body are invited to participate in the comfort of the needy: the stranger whose body is uncomfortable because it is not familiar to others, the sick whose body appears abnormal or threatening, the prisoner whose body is deprived of stimulation and community, the hungry's grotesque physical features.

God hides and bids

Compassion for the least of people is not mere theory or sentiment. It is highly practical. Acts of mercy are actions anyone can offer, from feeding to sheltering, from clothing to giving drink, from visiting to welcoming, from educating to counseling, from consoling to praying.

One common mistake we often make, though, is to offer our help in a general manner rather than through a specific one. "If there is anything I can do," we say, "let me know." In essence, we diffuse our responsibility. A universal offer lacks the specificity of passion. In fact, Matthew Fox remarks that in the story of the good Samaritan Jesus defines compassion in terms of particular actions—"going to him, binding up wounds, pouring on oil, putting him on his beast, bringing him to an inn, and caring for him."

God's love is hidden in the cross. And it is hidden in our human crosses. Luther said, ". . . Christ was powerless on the cross, and yet there he performed his mightiest work and conquered sin, death, world, hell, devil, and all evil." [2] So God's love is mightiest in our weakness too—even the weakness of our physical frame. The cross of Christ assures us that God really works for us where everything apparently denies him. Kazoh Kitamori suggests, "God becomes *immanent* in these realities of pain: he says, 'for I was hungry.' " God hides in his own suffering. He hides in our own troubles. And he hides in the bodily needs of the least of people. Such is the way of the cross. For Jesus, described as having "nowhere to lay his head," identifies with the stranger, crying "I thirst" from the cross with the thirsty, fasting in the wilderness with the hungry, healing the leper and the deaf with the sick, stripped to linen cloths with the naked, and dying a physical death with our whole physical dilemma.

God does not love disembodied people, as if our souls are precious or good and our bodies neutral or bad. If indeed the gift of the resurrection is that of a new body, a glorious one, incorruptible, and immortal, it says much about God's concern for the physical and material side of life.

Think, then, of the least of people around and beyond your own lives: the refugee, the physically disabled, the migrant worker, the unattractive, the ill. In their darkness God hides and bids us come. God who is rich in mercy has revealed his comfort to us and leads us to a like compassion for others, where we meet him again in human needs. He invites us to be everywhere with him, compassionate as he is compassionate. Strangely, he invites us to the place of his presence hidden in the dark night of the needy. "But if any one has the world's goods and sees his brother in need," writes John, "yet closes his heart against him, how does God's love abide in him?" [3:17]

The light of the glory of God hidden in the darkness of human need? Like a good storyteller, God thickens the plot, surging back and forth. He transfers us from the darkness of sin to the saving light of the gospel of Jesus Christ, and then throws us, light in hand, into the darkness where God is.

"Welcome one another, therefore, as Christ has welcomed you, for the glory of God" [Rom. 15:7]. Welcome to glory! Surprised?—so were those in Matthew 25.

"Now is my soul troubled. And what shall I say? 'Father, save me from this hour'? No, for this purpose I have come to this hour. Father, glorify thy name." Then a voice came from heaven, "I have glorified it, and I will glorify it again." The crowd standing by heard it and said that it had thundered. Others said, "An angel has spoken to him." Jesus answered, "This voice has come for your sake, not mine. Now is the judgment of this world, now shall the ruler of this world be cast out; and I, when I am lifted up from the earth, will draw all men to myself." He said this to show by what death he was to die. The crowd answered him, "We have heard from the law that the Christ remains for ever. How can you say that the Son of man must be lifted up? Who is this Son of man?" Jesus said to them, "The light is with you for a little longer. Walk while you have the light, lest the darkness overtake you; he who walks in the darkness does not know where he goes. While you have the light, believe in the light, that you may become sons of light."

JOHN 12:27-36

STRANGE GLORY

The hidden yes

God hides: "Truly, thou art a God who hidest thyself, O God of Israel, the Savior" [Isa. 45:15]. God comes at unexpected hours: "Take heed, watch; for you do not know when the time will come" [Mark 13:33]. God delays: "My way is hid from the Lord, and my right is disregarded by my God" [Isa. 40:27]. God has a will of his own: "I will be gracious to whom I will be gracious, and will show mercy on whom I will show mercy" [Exod. 33:19]. God works in opposites, hiding his grace under wrath and his gifts under troubles: "For God has consigned all men to disobedience, that he may have mercy upon all" [Rom. 11:32]. God has a storehouse of surprises: "From of old no one has heard or perceived by the ear, no eye has seen a God besides thee, who works for those who wait for him" [Isa. 64:4]. God's wisdom is unlike ours: "For the wisdom of this world is folly with God" [1 Cor. 3:19]. God is steeped in mystery: "For who has known the mind of the Lord, or who has been his counselor?" [Rom. 11:34]. God has disguises and masks: "While they were talking and discussing together, Jesus himself drew near and went with them. But their eyes were kept from recognizing him" [Luke 24:15-16].

Small wonder, therefore, that Luther mentions that "God insofar as he has hidden himself" is no concern of ours. If, like Moses, we cannot see his naked power and glory, surely we cannot, as Paul says, fully understand his mind and will. God comes "clothed in his word." We concern ourselves with "the God who has become flesh." As the writer of Hebrews remarks, God speaks to us "by a Son" who "reflects the glory of God" [1:2-3]. He comes to us in the masks and clothing of word and faith, in Baptism and the sacrament. Whatever God does, wills, thinks, or is *in himself* is not ours to know. We know him only *in his relationship* with us, that is, in what he promises and gives. By direct searching we will never find him. And why he chooses to hide himself, we will never know or understand. For what reasons God covers his steadfast love under its opposites—cross, suffering, wrath, troubles, weakness, pain, darkness—exceeds reason and comprehension. By *nature* we trust what we see; by *faith* we hold fast to the deep and hidden 'yes' under and above the no, trusting firmly in God's word. God dresses out in promises, not in power. But, of course, *we* want to dress him up in high fashion, dashing colors, and unquestionable taste. We associate him with the good and bright, the glittering and glamorous, the spectacular and big splash. Left to our choices, God would be outfitted with power and apparelled with class and, while he would not be a golden calf, to all appearances he would be a slick-looking executive.

The prince and the tramp

Two illustrations reveal something, at least, of this hidden God. The first is Søren Kierkegaard's story of the prince pursuing his beloved. The prince used the guise of a peasant to woo her. While never ceasing to be a prince, he hid his identity so that she would love him for what he was and not for the role he played. Power, like beauty, is skin deep. It is a veneer, a surface. God, too, hides in the flesh of Jesus Christ to manifest his character, his heart, and his compassion, never ceasing to be God.

The second illustration is a comic film—*City Lights*—featuring Charlie Chaplin. Charlie is a tramp, a tragic/comic figure. On one occasion a rich man, intoxicated, rewards Charlie financially. Later Charlie faces the rich man's rejection, as the plutocrat sobers up. Worse yet, the rich man charges Charlie with the theft of his money, even though the tramp received it as a gift from the drunken tycoon. With the police in pursuit, Charlie manages to give the money to a blind girl for eye surgery. Finally the tramp is caught and incarcerated.

After serving his prison sentence, the tramp returns to the world. Thinking that her benefactor is a tall, dark, and handsome figure, the blind girl does not notice Charlie. Sadly, she scorns the little man as he passes by her flower shop. At the end she suddenly discovers that the tramp, unkempt and forlorn, is her rescuer. Using her sense of blindness—touch—she feels his arm and face, speaking softly and incredibly, "You!"

These two accounts do not explain the hiddenness of God, but they point to it. God hides in order to reveal. He employs aliases and hideouts to convey his truth. Disguised, he teases and tests us. With ambiguity, he keeps us guessing. Clothed in promises, he incites our courage. Through paradox, he stretches our imagination. God will be God only on his generous terms and through his unexpected ways.

For this purpose

Maybe now we can make some sense of Jesus' words recorded in John 12. In the Fourth Gospel we find no report of agony and prayer in Gethsemane. The human struggle against death at age thirty-three and on a cross takes a different twist. "Now is my soul troubled," lamented Jesus, "And what shall I say?" He turned immediately to the human issue of asking the Father to

65

save him from this hour. But Jesus cast aside the idea: "No, for this purpose I have come to this hour." Instead, he uttered an invocation, saying, "Father, glorify thy name." Again, as at other great moments in Jesus' life—his baptism, the transfiguration on the mountaintop, and his decision to go to Jerusalem—the voice of God was audible: "I have glorified it, and I will glorify it again." Jesus identified the glorification with judgment, the fall of the ruler of this world, and his own death.

Confusion pervaded the crowd. With disbelief they retorted, "We have heard from the law that the Christ remains for ever. How can you say that the Son of Man must be lifted up?" The prophet Daniel attributes "an everlasting dominion, which shall not pass away" to the son of man [Dan. 7:14]. And before him, Isaiah lyricizes that "of the increase of his government and of peace there will be no end" [Isa. 9:7]. Besides this testimony of the Hebrew scriptures, a number of messianic expectations contradicted the idea that the son of man would die, implied in Jesus' words about being lifted up. The Zealots, for instance, hoped for political restoration and anticipated military action under the Messiah's leadership to secure independence from Rome's domination. The Pharisees looked for the supremacy of God's people in an ideal community under the rule of the Messiah. The alarmists in Hebrew society envisioned a great catastrophe occurring with the Messiah's coming. Neither Jewish tradition nor common expectations prepared the people for the strange entry of the Messiah into human life, especially hanging on a cross—the form of execution, no less, of the despised Romans.

So instinctively, the crowd's bewilderment led to the question, "Who is this son of man?" The son of man dying? No display of power? No demonstration or establishment of a holy paradise on earth? No hint even of a juncture in history? Dead heroes don't succeed. Martyrs are admirable, but hardly inspirational for the long haul.

From a modern point of view, Jesus' answer is a ghostly gen-

66

erality, a three- or four-liner fit for a public event where no one is to be offended or amazed. It sounds significant but is innocuous: "While you have the light, believe in the light, that you may become sons of light." As far as the original listeners were concerned, it certainly struck no monumental impression. Sun gods, star-light, star-bright—years of comparison between the Holy One and the light had been in effect. But now they wanted some crisp identification: a driver's license, two credit cards, and the correct street address and telephone number. Jesus' one credential, "he had done so many signs before them" [12:37], failed to turn the tide of their confidence toward Jesus. We could imagine someone in the crowd brusquely saying, "Cut out the oriental philosophy! We have heard it before. Show us your *vitae,* letters of references, and plan for executing your messiahship." And another incredulous individual saying to friends, "He is the light?"

Lest we condemn the contemporaries of Jesus offhandedly, we need to remember that we are scarcely more perceptive and receptive. Jaded by two thousand years of Christianity, we have lost our appetite for both its sharp and sweet taste. For example, we believe that we capture the "light" with a few sanctuary candles; we think the strange glory of the crucifixion can be fully conveyed with a hand gesturing upon the forehead and chest. We equate walking in the light with a few inches of charity stepped off in the direction of the needy. And we pray with heightened attentiveness and hope when the pastor prays for our Aunt Sarah, as if she were more important to God than somebody who is related to some church member we don't even know and for whom we prayed last week. It's all too familiar, too routine, too flattened out, too comfortable. A light is shining in this shadowy world, in that foggy marriage, in other cloudy circumstances, and in our own darkness. But we see it through a dark glass. Maybe Annie Dillard, who writes with a bit of satire, catches what dullards we are when she says that we are raising tomatoes when we should be raising Cain.

The small things

We examined previously the "real presence" of Christ "in, with, and under" the disfigured, diseased, and divergent forms of the body. But the light of his presence there hardly dawns on us, just as it hardly enlightened some parts of the Christian church in the past. At one time, it is to be noted, the church expounded on the virtue of "holy pilgrimages" for the sick to visit shrines far away for miraculous recovery. Well-intentioned, no doubt, they still missed the light of the Great Physician right there in the life of the ill. Even Luther denounced the mentally feeble as "filled with Satan." The disabled were categorized as defective, dangerous, and inferior, without a thought as to how "disabled" Christ himself was when he was nailed to the cross.

Like our churchly antecedents, we too miss the light hidden in human disability. And consider also the same hiddenness of Christ in the statement, "where two or three are gathered in my name, there am I in the midst of them" [Matt. 18:20]. We assume that anything with size has impact and influence. Numbers prove. Surrounded as we are by an *inflated* economy, *more* people to every square mile than ever before, and the *multiplying* of options, we seldom stop to question the bigger is better formula. And yet, in the gathering of two or three hundred, Christ's presence may become more problematic. Surely a crowd has an intoxicating effect, leaving the mass in the state of greater suggestibility and with less personal responsibility. "Socially conditioned" or "acculturated"—whatever—we overlook the *spiritual* value of the gathering of two or three in the name of Christ. We are too busy with headcounts, an imperialistic type of mission work, and parish growth.

The light becomes diffuse over a wider area. Can we still imagine, then, that the light may shine brighter and clearer in pairs and triads? Could it be that we expect the glory of God only when desired numbers are present? Is Christ not hidden in the little conversation of friends, the intimate consolation of one-to-one, the small gifts shared by companions? For if anything, the cross means that truth needs only a majority of *one*. Truth cannot be manufactured by a giant corporation. Maybe we need to take a good, hard look at the relationship between the truth and the twos and threes gathered together: things like private confession, two becoming "one flesh," a mother's promise to a child at birth and during infancy, being a "soul friend" to others, and giving hospitality. If indeed we are to become children of the light, we need to become brothers and sisters and cousins to others who belong to the Father.

Strange but strong

Strange glory! It is indirect lighting—in the least of people, in the two or three gathered together. Jesus reveals the Father in death and the cross, he manifests the heart of God by suffering and pain, he opens up the "secret and hidden wisdom of God" through agony and defeat. "Now is my soul troubled. . . ." Glorification is through crucifixion. Revelation is through hiddenness. Life is through death. Light is through darkness. Truth is through those basic units of life.

Despite our flattened and familiar version of Christianity and despite our impulsive penchant for numbers and size, the light shines in our darkness. But the light is always a *gift,* never available by the strength of reason, the force of will, the perception of a sign, the command of numbers. The light lies beyond our control. The light neither dawns in the east nor sets in the west; the light neither perches at noon nor dips at midday. That is light seen from the perspective of the earth. The light is an everlasting light, shining even though the hemisphere of our lives spins away from its presence. "Love never ends."

To the Jews the light encompassed a depth of meaning; to see was to be alive, to be led by the light was to be pushed, pulled, prodded, and plopped down the path of truth. To receive the light was to receive salvation. But these people stood there waiting for a blaze of glory, just as Moses before them requested the full view of God's face. No twinkle, twinkle little star for these people—they longed for the recognizable Messiah, a clear statement of identity, maybe a *skekinah*—the bright cloud of the exodus that led the people of Israel out of Egypt.

" 'Father, save me from this hour'? No, for this purpose I have come to this hour! Father, glorify thy name." And what is that name? "I will be gracious to whom I will be gracious" [Exod. 33:19]. That's the glory! That's the light! That's the word! God wants us to know him by his *name*. Forget the signs and numbers, the assumptions and traditions, the appearances and sights. Listen to the name: *grace*. What a strange glory! But what a strong promise!

As a hart longs for flowing streams, so longs my soul for thee, O God. My soul thirsts for God, for the living God. When shall I come and behold the face of God? My tears have been my food day and night, while men say to me continually, "Where is your God?" These things I remember, as I pour out my soul: how I went with the throng, and led them in procession to the house of God, with glad shouts and songs of thanksgiving, a multitude keeping festival. Why are you cast down, O my soul, and why are you disquieted within me? Hope in God; for I shall again praise him, my help and my God. My soul is cast down within me, therefore I remember thee from the land of Jordan and of Hermon, from Mount Mizar. Deep calls to deep at the thunder of thy cataracts; all thy waves and thy billows have gone over me. By day the Lord commands his steadfast love; and at night his song is with me, a prayer to the God of my life. I say to God, my rock: "Why hast thou forgotten me? Why go I mourning because of the oppression of the enemy?" As with a deadly wound in my body, my adversaries taunt me, while they say to me continually, "Where is your God?" Why are you cast down, O my soul, and why are you disquieted within me? Hope in God; for I shall again praise him, my help and my God.

PSALM 42

DIVINE GRACE
THE EXPERIENCE OF BEING
DELIVERED FROM EXPERIENCE

Caught in the middle

The midday demon is boredom. The three o'clock nag, as me-
dieval tradition put it, consists of melancholy, helplessness, dol-
drums, and despair. And no one, says Luther, "enjoys our fretting
and groaning" more than the devil. During his later years, Luther
scanned his life and remarked that his greatest harm had come
from sorrow. Hence, he advised, "you young fellows must guard
against sorrow. . . . It damages the body." Questions about mental
sanity crop up as well. Verging on a death-wish, a depressed
Luther could still say, "If I go mad, God will remain sane and
Christ my Lord will be my wisdom." More dangerous yet, heavy
sorrow leads to the despair of God's grace *(fidei tentatio)*.[1]

Luther used the word *Anfechtung* for the troubles he endured
—his doubt, panic, desperation, anguish, despair, anxiety, and
painful struggles. According to our reason and senses, these
appear to contradict the presence of God. But God sees our
affliction as only a point, a moment, a drop, a spark. Our
troubles look far different to God than they do to us. Through
faith, we see troubles as God does, in a different way from our

73

own senses. Faith is "the conviction of things not seen." Even though our feelings and experiences contradict the reality of God's presence and promise, faith waits for the work of the Holy Spirit. All through life we undergo the tension between sorrow, deeply felt, and comfort, graciously given. Heinrich Bornkamm, for example, writes:

> ...Luther applied the old military term *Anfechtung* to this distress of the heart. For these are not merely questions of weary doubts and misgivings; they are attacks of an enemy skilled in fighting *(Fechten)*. For our comfort Luther informed us that in this respect we are only sharing the experiences of Christ, who emptied this cup to the dregs, and that in this way God purifies and refines our faith and our trust in Him. 'I did not learn my theology at one time, but I had to meditate deeper and deeper. Then my *Anfechtung* carried me thither. For this cannot be acquired without experience'.... Because Luther had experienced the blessing of doubts and *Anfechtung*, he called them 'God's embraces.' And faith must transform the terrifying aspects of these painful embraces of the hidden God into the gracious countenance of the revealed God.[2]

That's precisely where the forty-second Psalm is—hanging between the painful embraces and gracious countenance.

Longings and limits

The psalm begins with a common experience: a soul longing and thirsting for God. It could be the soul of a teenager crying out from the pit of loneliness. It could be the soul of an elderly person who is wracked with pain. Maybe it's the soul of the divorcee, hurting from obvious rejection. Perhaps the soul belongs to a parent who is dumbfounded about a chlid's neglect and ungratefulness. "When shall I come and behold the face of God?" We are not strangers to this sentiment. For one thing, we encountered it in the story of Moses in Exodus. Second, we ask the question ourselves. The longing soul has come up against the limitations of reality. Notice the psalmist's feelings, tears rolling down a sad face: "Why are you cast down, O my soul, and why are you disquieted within me?" There is a sorrow, "Why go I mourning," and the mockery of others, "Where is your God?" At the same time, the thirsty soul finds some living water: the steadfast love of the Lord, the remembrance of "glad shouts and songs of thanksgiving," and God, the rock and the helper. Under stress and strain, the psalmist struggles, in a faithful manner, to transform the painful embraces of the hidden God, "Why hast thou forgotten me?," into the gracious countenance of the revealed God, "By day the Lord commands his steadfast love." The same predicament is ours. We stand between human feelings and gracious reality, between mournful experiences and comforting word, between human limitations and spiritual longings, between sight and faith.

What we are confronting is the relationship between experience and faith. For the moment, let us leave the experience of sorrow and turn attention to the experience of complete joy. Certainly the psalmist is far from emotional elation. But we need to examine the other extreme of human experience, for a moment anyway, simply because of its prevalence today. We make the simple and clear deduction that "feeling good" or "experiencing delight" signals God's activity. No one would deny the "joyful noise" or "Be of good cheer" motif in the life of a Christian. In fact, Luther said that the law is not kept if it is not done in joy. And none would contest the suggestion that if we are redeemed we could certainly look like it more often, including its joyful aspects. Don't we yawn sometimes when we say, "Let's have a party!" Then, too, let us speak of celebration, joy, and festivals. But notice *how* we speak of it—with such austerity and dead seriousness or a bit of pulpit-pounding.

What we want is some emotion and enthusiasm in our Christian life. But sweet feelings do not produce God's presence or make his promises full-blown. Faith in the steadfast love of God is not *dependent* on any particular kind of experience, whether we label experience "meditation" or "born again" or "celebration." Faith is not the same as a rhapsodic experience, an overpowering turning point, or flamboyant feeling states. That makes the graciousness of God dependent on the experience, especially an effective one. In the biblical record, we see case after case where *experience is lacking but faith is waiting.* To Mary, the angel announces the birth of the Messiah. There is no evidence that she joined the local Religious Aglow Group for Pregnant Women. Amazed, she questions, "How shall this be?" [Luke 1:34] The disciples walking to Emmaus, not recognizing the man who had joined them on their path, discovered in the breaking of bread later in the day that the stranger was no one less than the resurrected Lord. Only *after* the experience were they able to discuss the experience: "Did not our hearts burn within us?" [Luke 24:32] In the parable of Dives and Lazarus, Lazarus implores Abraham to warn the living about the torture of hell. What is the response? The brothers of Lazarus do not need any experience, for they have the Law and the Prophets. Endlessly the *initiative* of God's gracious action is emphasized.

While faith is not dependent on experience, it is surely experienced. But the presence and promise of God are seen from the rear—that is, after the experience itself. Faith waits, neither having all in hand nor knowing in full. Experience does not establish faith. Experience flows from faith, is a result of faith, and is the school of the Holy Spirit. Faith and experience cross paths at the point of trust. Trust is knowing in part yet taking the chance on God who knows in full.

There is a cartoon depicting several men leaving the scene of the crucifixion of Christ. One of the men is saying to the others, "That didn't do a thing for me." The implication, of course, is that we expect some emotional payoff. What better dividend than happiness, high delight, and upturned smiles!

W. H. Auden captured this theme of being enchanted, or wanting to be enchanted by God. He wrote:

Christ did not enchant men; He demanded that they believe in Him. Except on one occasion, the Transfiguration. For a brief while,

Peter, James, and John were permitted to see Him in His glory. For that brief while they had no need of faith. The vision vanished, and the memory of it did not prevent them from all forsaking Him when He was arrested, or Peter from denying that he had ever known Him.[3]

No human experience guarantees anything. Furthermore, we never relinquish the pride that wishes to assert itself. We can project our subjective feelings onto the Holy Spirit. In the process, longing for stimulation and benevolence, we neglect the awe, the marvel, the sheer surprise of the free gift of God—grace. The experience is never the full reality; the feeling is never the complete story. And this is true whether the experience is boredom or elation, the feeling exciting or dull.

Experience and faith

Leaving the digression, we return to the lower end of the spectrum and the issue of sorrow and God's presence. With crying towel in hand, the psalmist wrestles with the facts. As our therapists and clinicians say, the psalmist "honors his feelings." Sick of soul, he cries and complains. In the fashion of Job, he prepares to argue his case before the Almighty: his soul is locked in silence, others throw taunts at him, and God has forgotten him. He does not boast of his sufferings. Sufferings destroy. Sorrow bears all the dimensions of the demonic. It is possessive and all-consuming; it preoccupies and presses against the mind. Suffering itself has no merit. But the occasion of sorrow raises questions of its own. In one sense, pain is a teacher without which we cannot do. Putting aside for the moment the excruciating experience and the inner state of anguish, the psalmist acknowledges the goodness of God—"my help," "my God," and "my rock." He stands as a counterpart to the New Testament figure who utters, "I believe; help my unbelief!" [Mark 9:24] We truly appreciate these biblical characters, because we know

77

and contend with the immense paradox of faith. While sorrow seemingly denies God, we realize nevertheless that with him all things are possible. This, in Søren Kierkegaard's words, is the "eternally certain antidote to despair."

Like the psalmist, we must forever pass from *this* experience —horrible as it may appear or feel—to *that* faith which recognizes the reality of God's grace hidden under its opposite. Grace is hidden under our sorrow. Compassion is hidden under our grief. Goodness is hidden under our misfortune. Steadfast love is hidden under our shaky fears. Mercy is hidden under our troubles. Peace is hidden under our anxiety. No wonder that Luther could brazenly assert: "God is known only in suffering." He knew that God's grace is made perfect whenever we sit "in pious ignorance and mental darkness" and remain sitting "without understanding, without feeling, without thinking." Luther's idea of "blind faith" is defined in his statement: "faith is a sort of darkness which sees nothing. . . . Yet the Christ of whom faith takes hold is sitting in this darkness." [4] So Luther opposed the theology of glory because of the *starting* point: from the visible to the invisible, from below to above, from good feelings to grace, from a grand experience to God's presence, from a dramatic event to God's power, from the obvious to the incomprehensible God. Faith begins grace downward, not ground upward. Luther suggests that faith is not seeing the visible and seeing what is invisible. Faith is imaginative; faith is courage.

Perhaps now you can understand the digression we made as we considered the experience of prosperity or the feeling of happiness and equating them with God's grace. The more we hunger for the experience or feeling that we deem appropriate for God's presence and faith's certainty, the less we will ever come to know them. No human experience is the *cause* of grace. Grace is always a gift; the effect or response is trust. "Trust is born of care." The initiative of God is the grace of God. So whenever we desire to experience, feel, know, or see God based on our senses, we miss him. Grace is sufficient when it is not subject to our demands.

An invitation to remember

Look at the psalmist, distraught and distressed. What did he do? He *remembered*. He reflected on *other* experiences. He realized that a whole field of experiences have existed. For a moment he forgot this one overwhelming, possessive, demanding, and demonic experience: life is a whole. We do not need to minimize our misery or to maximize our merriment to trust God. He is hidden in the suffering and cross of Jesus Christ. And he is hidden in ours too, regardless of our feelings and all appearances.

"Do this in remembrance of me." And as often as we do it in remembrance of him, we "proclaim the Lord's death" [1 Cor. 11:26]. He is hidden "in, with, and under" the bread and wine of Holy Communion. No human feeling, no human action, no human experience, no human reasoning make him present. Recall the exact words of the psalmist: "the Lord commands his steadfast love." It is there. It is irreversible. It cannot be meddled with or modified. The grace of God is uncaused and unsolicited, unprecedented and unlimited. The grace of God is God finding the lost sinner; the grace of God is God releasing the sinner from the entrapment of evil. Grace is God's initiative. Grace is God's yes. He promises it and delivers it. As for us, we remember it and receive it, even hidden under bread and wine or the cross and suffering.

In his *Large Catechism,* Luther states that the ones who most need the sacrament of the Lord's Supper are (1) those who feel they do not *need* it and (2) those who feel they are *unworthy* to receive it. The feelings are consequences of the need. The essence of it all is *need*. We need the grace of God. Yet the need does not produce the gift. It is already there. We are *invited* to the feast: "Take eat!" and "Take drink!" And he is worthy to receive this grace who trusts in the *word,* the *promise*—"given and shed for you for the forgiveness of sins."

Waiting on God

Even while the psalmist remembers the experience of shouts and thanksgiving for God, he is *now* unable to appeal to any like *experience at hand.* Waiting with a disquieted heart and on an unknown path, he trusts and praises God's goodness nevertheless. What a difficult discipline for the human soul: standing at the point of intense need, remaining stubbornly and longingly at the empty center precisely when the hunger reaches its zenith, enduring patiently the mysterious silence. Bent and tormented, we are tempted to move too fast, to prime our emotional well, and to form an experience of the presence of God. But grace is the experience of being delivered from experience. For if grace is a free gift, God acts freely. He will not remain aloof and remote forever. To hunger for the experience is to wait for the freedom of God. But when we demand the experience, we forget the *free gift.* Experience can become an idol—a certainty of God based on our need to know, a grace centered on our human sentiment. To be a "free" gift, grace will always come as a surprise, without prompting, and as revelation. Listen to Julius Lester:

> What God does is His business and if He thinks I need to have a reason, He'll provide it. If not, He won't. In either instance, my way is clear: To be a vessel for the Divine Will. I am to be Abraham, carrying my son up the mountain to be sacrificed, not questioning why God commands it, or even hesitating in my step. . . .
> . . . . I must take to heart the warnings of St. John of the Cross about religious emotionalism. It is only in the dark night of the soul, when all signs of God's love and presence are absent, that one can be purged of religious experiences based in the senses. To even desire emotional religious experiences is spiritual gluttony, according to the Spanish mystic, making an end out of means. If we need and seek emotional religious experiences, we will never live a life of faith, which means to love God when He refuses to make Himself known, to trust His will even when it seems to bring us only suffering.[5]

The psalmist's sorrow is every bit a part of faith in God.

Suffering is ingrained in the message of grace and embedded in the image of the cross. It is reserved for the eyes of faith. How could we show off our religious experiences or boast of our affections in view of the crucified who died in his weakness for our sin? Nothing can separate us from the love of God revealed in Jesus Christ who suffers with us. And waiting trust calls for no experience of this kind or that, no preconditions for the reality of God to be real. "My rock," shouts the psalmist, solid in his promises and goodness, steadfast in love, and immovable from the ground of mercy. Or, in the words of Hans Küng, "God's love does not protect us *against* all suffering. But it protects us *in* all suffering, hidden though it be."

Moreover, faith—even though not dependent on experience—can still be experienced in all aspects of life. To the higher medicines, Luther adds such prescriptions as "the mutual conversation and consolation of the brethren," a wise counselor, the fellowship of the church, music, the love of a woman (and we would add, a man), eating, dancing, joking, manual work, and watching children play. Above all, though, "hold him to his promises," Luther says, like this promise, "given and shed for you for the forgiveness of sin." Grace is never too little, even when we let the demon of sorrow grow too big. "Hope in God" (Ps. 42:11).

For the word of the cross is folly to those who are perishing, but to us who are being saved it is the power of God. For it is written, "I will destroy the wisdom of the wise, and the cleverness of the clever I will thwart." Where is the wise man? Where is the scribe? Where is the debater of this age? Has not God made foolish the wisdom of the world? For since, in the wisdom of God, the world did not know God through wisdom, it pleased God through the folly of what we preach to save those who believe. For Jews demand signs and Greeks seek wisdom, but we preach Christ crucified, a stumbling block to Jews and folly to Gentiles, but to those who are called, both Jews and Greeks, Christ the power of God and the wisdom of God. For the foolishness of God is wiser than men, and the weakness of God is stronger than men.

For consider your call, brethren; not many of you were wise according to worldly standards, not many were powerful, not many were of noble birth; but God chose what is foolish in the world to shame the wise, God chose what is weak in the world to shame the strong, God chose what is low and despised in the world, even things that are not, to bring to nothing things that are, so that no human being might boast in the presence of God. He is the source of your life in Christ Jesus, whom God made our wisdom, our righteousness and sanctification and redemption; therefore, as it is written, "Let him who boasts, boast of the Lord."

1 CORINTHIANS 1:18-31

THE FOOLISHNESS OF GOD

The foolish cross

Fools for Christ's sake! Remember Paul's description of the apostles? They are fools because they are "last of all," comparable to "men sentenced to death," and "the refuse of the world." The apostles are weak, held in disrepute, buffeted, and homeless. Instead of cursing those who complain against them, the apostles bless. Slandered, they nevertheless try to conciliate. If anything, these early apostles exemplify in their lives how a life of faith involves risks, uncertainties, and adversaries.

But Paul speaks of another kind of foolishness too—the foolishness of the cross. To the Jews, the cross is a scandal. In their law it is written: "a hanged man is accursed of God" [Deut. 21:23]. The crucifixion of a Messiah is easily rejected. Who wants more suffering? Haven't we had plenty of tragedy and enough violence? The cross and suffering remain as twin absurdities, even more so for Jews, with the tradition of their law. Moreover, the Jews were looking for signs. If God were to visit his people, striking and startling events would mark the moment. Certainly none anticipated the shame of ignoble suffering. For other reasons, the Greeks considered the cross sheer folly. God was detached and remote from human life. He could not feel. The passion of Christ seemed ridiculous, for the Greeks believed that if God could be *affected,* he could be changed by mere mortals. Wisdom or the mind, not passion or feeling, stood supreme. What foolishness to preach Christ crucified, as if God could suffer and feel pain!

Of course Paul was citing the fact that for all the wisdom of the world, for all its traditions, and for all its tastes and assumptions, the world still staggers in its search for God. The gospel is unpalatable to our expectations, whether they be hungerings for flashy miracles or flowery words. Like the first century Jew and Greek, the crucifixion is a joke, a hoax, or a fool's word. And it is no less ludicrous today than it was then. Trying to imagine himself near the events of that Friday's crucifixion on Calvary, W. H. Auden wrote:

Just as we were all, potentially, in Adam when he fell, so we were all, potentially, in Jerusalem on that first Good Friday before there was an Easter, a Pentecost, a Christian, or a Church. It seems to me worth while asking ourselves who we should have been and what we should have been doing. None of us, I'm certain, will imagine himself as one of the Disciples, cowering in agony of spiritual despair and physical terror. Very few of us are big wheels enough to see ourselves as Pilate, or good churchmen enough to see ourselves as a member of the Sanhedrin. In my most optimistic mood I see myself as a Hellenized Jew from Alexandria visiting an intellectual friend. We are walking along, engaged in philosophical argument. Our path takes us past the base of Golgotha. Looking up, we see an all too familiar sight—three crosses surrounded by a jeering crowd. Frowning with prim distaste, I say, "It's disgusting the way the mob enjoys such things. Why can't the authorities execute criminals humanely and in private by giving them hemlock to drink, as they did with Socrates?" Then, averting my eyes from the disagreeable spectacle, I resume our fascinating discussion about the nature of the True, the Good, and the Beautiful.[1]

Are we not Hellenized Jews from Los Angeles, Dallas, or Atlanta? We hurl our disgust against the mob in their perverse delight over the misery of others. We answer their clownish taunts with our civilized disapproval. With our sensibilities offended we deplore the lack of good taste and humanness among those who wield the sword. Traumatized for a second, we resume our own fascination with the free enterprise system, designer clothing, the delicious quiche, the electronic toy, and the spit and shine of modern tidiness. We may not, after all, call it foolishness. Our crosses dangle in sterling silver from our necks and stand stately before our eyes in the chancel. We have taken the cross and made it part of "our fascination . . . about . . . the True, the Good, and the Beautiful." As soon as we eliminate its scandal, though, we remove all of its nonsense, unexpectedness, and strangeness. No wonder Julius Lester places us in a second parody, saying,

Evil is. That is the unmistakable message of the Holocaust. Look and see what evil is capable of. But we sit on pews, our eyes riveted on the murder of the Son of God, and say our rosaries, pray at the Stations of the Cross, sing Amazing Grace and jog up and down the aisles. We cannot see evil because we want only the good.[2]

The fine print

What are we going to do with the foolishness of God? Tame its truth? Make it reasonable? Simplify it? Remove its scandal? Bury it in a liturgy?

At the opposite end of the scale, we could take advantage of the folly and turn to the zany, the antic, and the offbeat. Why not the Greatest Show on Earth: beer-and-pretzel communion, clowns and more clowns in the service, humming the hymns on kazoos? If some can make a profit out of the gospel at least we can have some fun with it!

If the offbeat and comic seem too disgraceful, why not dull the gospel with shine? "Have faith, then expect miracles!" But "have faith"—like "earn grace"—is a contradiction. Since grace is an unmerited gift, how can we bargain for it? Furthermore, since faith is always not having completely, how can we possess it? Then, try this one: "Think it possible!" Positive Mental Attitude—it has been the gospel of sales meetings from the high-rise Holiday Inn to the metal frame cubicle housing the vacuum cleaner business—the time-tested motivational psychology for excitement and success. But we do wonder why, for example, the density of the disciples in discerning the words of Jesus caused him to offer no ripples of advice concerning positive thinking. Case Study A: "No, Master," Peter said, "you are not going to Jerusalem to become a victim and to die." A stern rebuke follows with the injunction, "Get behind me, Satan!" There are no allusions to PMA, such as, "Come on now, Peter, think big, think positively, think 'yes.'" What we hear is very negative, a judgment. Case Study B: "Who will be the greatest in the kingdom of heaven, Lord?" a pair of eager brothers ask. What do we hear? Not this—"Atta' way to go, you sons of Zebedee. Good thinking. Like your attitude. Pound that door of possibility." But this—the greatest will be the least. Case Study C: When the disciples asked Jesus to teach them how to pray, Jesus did not turn around and say, "I'll do even more. I'll teach you how to pray and be a success."

When we "shine" the gospel, we dull it. When we "polish" the folly so that it glistens as wisdom, we lose it. To expect miracles or to think positively, with any conditions, is to tamper with the incomprehensible, hidden God. If faith is to trust the promise of God in spite of all *appearances,* it is also to trust in spite of all *attitudes* and *thoughts.* Every attempt to hang conditions on the gospel is an attempt to drape signs and wisdom over its foolishness. Faith receives its full strength from Christ's complete weakness. God brings "to nothing things that are," including any hint or suggestion of human boasting. Annie Dillard paints the foolishness of God with vivid strokes:

There is not a guarantee in the world. Oh your needs are guaranteed, your needs are absolutely guaranteed by the most stringent of warranties, in the plainest, truest words: knock; seek; ask. But you must read the fine print. "Not as the world giveth, give I unto you." That's the catch. If you can catch it it will catch you up, aloft, up to any gap at all, and you'll come back, for you will come back, transformed in a way you may not have bargained for—dribbling and crazed. The waters of separation, however lightly sprinkled, leave indelible stains. Did you think, before you were caught, that you needed, say, life? Do you think you will keep your life, or anything else you love? But no. Your needs are all met. But not as the world giveth. You see the needs of your spirit met whenever you have asked, and you have learned that the outrageous guarantee holds. You see the creatures die, and you know you will die. And one day it occurs to you that you have finally understood that you're dealing with a maniac.[3]

Infatuated with glossy headlines, we easily neglect the "fine print." We do not get caught because we are caught up in our own enterprises. On the cloth of the most positive thought and miracle—expecting faith, there are "indelible stains"—filthy rags of righteousness, says one prophet.

The risk of love

The glory of God cannot be converted to glamor. How do we make "Christ crucified" pretty and pleasing? To be sure, crucifixion, pain, lowliness, and death are common embarrassments to us. We still want the safe (sign) and sane (wisdom) in our dealings with God. Glory reflected in the cross? Someone is pulling our leg. What do you want us to do, believe in a maniac? Indeed Paul mentions it—the very foolishness of what he preaches contains the word of salvation. What would we rather believe? Would God as President of the Universe be a more fitting image? Would God as Wall Street Banker do it for us? Would God as Brain Trust carry us through the day?

If we choose any of these images, we'd be in a hole—to be more exact—in the same bondage as ever. For what would we do with the parables? A father welcomes home his son. True, he is open to repentance. Nonetheless the son's motives for returning are mixed. Isn't there a bit of expediency? At least he will have three square meals like his father's servants enjoy. What a foolish action to accept this son without an explaining session, a good heart-to-heart talk, and some sign that the younger son has learned his lesson. Kill the fatted calf! If the father gets carried away in his foolishness, the elder brother holds the reins to reason. After all, Positive Mental Attitude has fastened him to exemplary obedience. The one *possibility,* though, that he never thought of was forgiveness, reconciliation, and love. Everything the father has is the elder's. What could be more possible? Perhaps just one thing—forgiveness for his brother. It is more than innocence or ignorance to believe in many possibilities for oneself and not see that the whole process leaves some things impossible for others.

The story of the laborers in the field expands the elder brother's brooding—that is, in terms of numbers. Each worker receives equal pay, but each has worked an unequal amount of time. "Do you," asks the employer, "begrudge my generosity?" Exactly! The labor contracts were signed, they were legal and just affairs. But the employer's *grace* sparks the quibbling. When another's possibilities exceed ours, we want to go back to the drawing board and even up the proportions.

These two parables describe the *glory* of God in acts of grace—"I will show mercy to whom I will show mercy." God's goodness is utterly foolish. God's abounding love is sheer absurdity. God's grace is a complete joke. In the crucified and forsaken Jesus "are hid all the treasures of wisdom and knowledge." It's a scandal because we want to start from *below,* see *directly,* and know *fully.* And yet, this is not *possible* if we start with grace. Basic to the meaning of mercy for the undeserving is the notion that help comes from outside of ourselves. Grace is God's will: it is self-expressive or free. Ultimately, the foolishness of God comes down to this: his grace "dawns" on us. We can neither storm the heavens, nor do the heavens force entry. Love has nothing to do with compulsion on our part or God's part. If one is gracious, one is never compulsive. Love is longsuffering, patient, and kind. Grace received is grace shouted: "Aha!" or "Amen!"

Maybe a human experience, though it is a limited illustration, can help us understand the "dawn of redeeming grace." Percy Knauth has written a book titled *A Season in Hell,* which is about succumbing to a vague but potent experience of depression. He says,

> Beside me, my wife stirred, then reached out a groping hand. She felt my shaking shoulders and suddenly came wide awake. I lifted my head and for the first time she saw my face as it had looked through all those solitary nights of recent months when I had fought alone in this attic room, away from her and our children because of the work that kept me in New York. Without a word, she took my head into her arms and rocked it on her breast while my tears flowed on and on until it seemed my soul was pouring out through my eye.
>
> This is the moment that I have to thank for the fact that I am still alive—that moment when I was cradled and comforted like the helpless infant I had become.

Like a fool, God hides his saving activity under its opposite. He makes alive by putting to death, he justifies by making us guilty, he shows mercy by placing us under the horrible reality of rejection. He makes us free by making us dependent—and it's that moment for which we are thankful for our life and hope, when he graciously cradles and comforts us. Luther tirelessly preached this foolishness of God, summarizing it in the following remark:

> And we, too, are constantly tempted to believe that God would abandon us and not keep his word; and in our hearts we begin thinking he is a liar. In short, God cannot be God unless he first becomes a devil. We cannot go to heaven unless we first go to hell. We cannot become God's children until we first become children of the devil.[5]

Thank God that he takes the risk to hide and conceal, to suffer and die, to become sin for us, to abandon us, to share our lot, to forgive us—and that he acted like a fool so that we might "become God's children."

. . . we are children of God, and if children, then heirs, heirs of God and fellow heirs with Christ, provided we suffer with him in order that we may also be glorified with him. I consider that the sufferings of this present time are not worth comparing with the glory that is to be revealed to us. For the creation waits with eager longing for the revealing of the sons of God; for the creation was subjected to futility, not of its own will but by the will of him who subjected it in hope; because the creation itself will be set free from its bondage to decay and obtain the glorious liberty of the children of God. We know that the whole creation has been groaning in travail together until now; and not only the creation, but we ourselves, who have the first fruits of the Spirit, groan inwardly as we wait for adoption as sons, the redemption of our bodies. For in this hope we were saved. Now hope that is seen is not hope. For who hopes for what he sees? But if we hope for what we do not see, we wait for it with patience. . . .

What then shall we say to this? If God is for us, who is against us? He who did not spare his own Son but gave him up for us all, will he not also give us all things with him? Who shall bring any charge against God's elect? It is God who justifies; who is to condemn? Is it Christ Jesus, who died, yes, who was raised from the dead, who is at the right hand of God, who indeed intercedes for us? Who shall separate us from the love of Christ? Shall tribulation, or distress, or persecution, or famine, or nakedness, or peril, or sword? As it is written, "For thy sake we are being killed all the day long; we are regarded as sheep to be slaughtered." No, in all these things we are more than conquerors through him who loved us. For I am sure that neither death, nor life, nor angels, nor principalities, nor things present, nor things to come, nor powers, nor height, nor depth, nor anything else in all creation, will be able to separate us from the love of God in Christ Jesus our Lord.

ROMANS 8:17-25, 31-39

GLORY, GLORY, HALLELUJAH

A noisy celebration

"Mine eyes have seen the glory of the coming of the Lord—Glory, glory, hallelujah!" Today our praises flow easily and fluently like the rippling stream. Shower-stall baritones can literally fall upon the words of the psalmist and "Make a joyful noise to the Lord." It is time for happy-hour shouting—at the top of our lungs—"Alleluia!" The pastor exclaims, "Christ is risen!" The worshipers respond, "Christ is risen indeed!" The last enemy is defeated, once and for all, and because Jesus lives we too shall live. "Glory, glory, hallelujah!" We toast with trumpets the very future which Baptism and faith opened up for us. Today we waste no energy booing the scrooges, the party-poopers, and other sad sacks. We forget the killjoys and give full attention to the songwriter: "He that goes forth weeping . . . shall come home with shouts of joy" (Ps. 126:6); to the Lord's promise: "So you have sorrow now, but I will see you again and your hearts will rejoice, and no one will take your joy from you" (John 16:22); and to the apostle Paul: "again I will say, Rejoice" (Phil. 4:4). We celebrate with cymbals this feast of victory for our God. Volcanic joy! Airy freedom! Triumphant hope! Christ the Lord shall reign forever. And nothing "will be able to separate us from the love of God in Christ Jesus our Lord." Nothing! Christ is risen!

Wait a minute! Hold it! Stop the music! What is all the shouting about? Is the Easter pageantry sweeping up our passions? Could this be nothing but a carnival of the spirit? A temptation to celebrate raw vitality, sensationalism? Are we simply letting off a little spiritual steam? Breaking the chains of routine with extraordinary exuberance? Religious people have a reputation for this kind of thing—excessive songs, far-fetched visions, and swollen emotions. Moreover, don't we usually protect ourselves against charges of zealousness and fanaticism—and disassociate ourselves from the impassioned? The super-enthusiasts embarrass us because we go about our religious life with poise and in low profile. Why, then, the sudden overflow of profuse praise?

We are begging for the obvious answer: "Christ Jesus, who died, yes who was raised from the dead" has made us "more than conquerors." Why not a bit of extreme festivity? But the resurrection is a many-splendored thing, far more than the singular self-interest of enduring beyond the grave. We are not attending the annual meeting of the Life after Life booster club. Are we glorifying ourselves under the pretense of rejoicing in the glory of the Lord? For Luther insisted that human beings insinuate themselves into everything, even God. If Ernest Becker is correct in saying, "What man really fears is not so much extinction, but extinction *with insignificance*," perhaps we are satisfying our appetites for prosperity and our desires for counting, for being significant. But some may sigh with an air of disgust over the prophetic penchant for dampening human spirits. Let's forget sin and its distortion effect. So what if we oversimplify or misunderstand the manifold meaning of the resurrection? Leave us alone and let us enjoy our childish or half-baked convictions.

Despite the yearning, understandably human and common, the

biblical text tugs at our resurrection perspectives—but not to gnaw away at this festival of faith; rather, to enlarge, deepen, and enrich both the festival and the faith. To see the coming of the glory of the Lord is to glimpse the most profound truth. Faith is not dependent on human will—on either our appetite or our desire, our longing or our will to live. Faith means that God holds us in the palm of his hand and as the apple of his eye. Faith is not based on having more, even if it is hallowed and divinely sanctioned. Life is a gift. Resurrection promises are gifts, all because God in his creative love delights in his creation. This delight has nothing whatsoever to do with the wishes of the creature for more life.

No private matter

To begin with, then, we attend to this idea of a *private* religion. Paul cites the "futility," the "bondage to decay," and the "groaning" of the whole creation. It "waits with eager longing" for the coming of the glory of the Lord. The cross and the resurrection constitute no one-dimensional solution to personal problems. The gospel is God's remedy for a futile, decaying, and groaning world. Paul proclaims a redemption not only to a biological species called *homo sapiens* but also to the subhuman world which "will be set free . . . and obtain the glorious liberty of the children of God." He's got the whole world in his hands, and on his mind, too, when he inserts the resurrection of Christ into history. The resurrection is God's *will* to liberate a decaying world from death; the resurrection is God's *initiative* to create anew a fallen world. Nowhere can we discern a highly private view which focuses on an individual's pining for more life, for counting for more than is possible for merely physical things, or for willful self-perpetuation. The resurrection is not our answer for our longing. The resurrection is God's answer to his own creative love for his whole creation. As part of that creation, we are beneficiaries as "we wait for adoption as sons, the redemption of our bodies." The resurrection is the story of the *gift* of God. "He who did not spare his own Son but gave him up for us all, will he not also give us all things with him?" It is not the fulfillment of our wishes, not even the hallowing of our deepest longings. We have no power to raise ourselves by our own willful bootstrings. If the resurrection depended on our will to die with distinction and significance, the spirit of it all would be desire, not hope. But desire can only run madly in pursuit of its compulsions. Desire centers on the self, the private being, with capacity for pleasure and happiness. The object of desire is the individual self. Desire is all-consuming. But once the desire is filled, it is removed, and there is nothing but emptiness —a return to futility, despair, and groaning. Take note, therefore, of Paul's description of the resurrection as that which produces hope and waiting "with patience." If anything, desire is impatient, a possessive drive. Hope waits and longs to receive.

A superabundance of private religion infiltrates the religious scene, as if God's only concern is for the personal salvation of souls. "God so loved the world," that is, his smallest creature as well as the crown of all creation, his people. God wills to set free every bit and piece of his world. We shrink the meaning of the resurrection to the self-coveting life. Yet God intends to save the whole world and to encompass all things—even to build a new heaven and a new earth.

But how can we shed the private view of things? As children we learned the nighttime prayer, "Now I lay me down to sleep, I pray the Lord my soul to keep. If I should die before I wake, I pray the Lord my soul to take." Then we learned hymn after hymn centered on "me-ism," such as, "Rock of Ages, Cleft for me" and "Jesus, Savior, pilot me." Lately we have heard with frequency the popular question, "Have you accepted Jesus Christ as your personal Savior?" without questioning its implications. God is not concerned with *our will* to endure, even though we cloak our self-interest with religious decisions, language, and works of piety. He is concerned, though, with his own *love* "in Christ Jesus our Lord" for the world. As we fret and dote on our own life extended beyond history, God cares for everything—even a man named Hinckley, a woman in Florida dubbed "Jane Doe," and a lot of others whose names we will never know. Even Buddy! Buddy who? Buddy is the character who works on your car, which he has towed to his garage from some desolate country road. You spend several days questioning Buddy's mechanical skills, bitterly disappointed that your trip ends up in Nowhereville. Perturbed, you cannot keep from wondering why in the world Jesus died and rose again for Buddy. What a mistake! But even Buddy!

So today we shout and praise God for the resurrection and our little glance into his glory, surely beyond our comprehension and far more imposing than a private affair, and thank him for a love that remembers each person and every thing and the whole creation. The resurrection marks the goal of *history*—and cannot be understood as simply the goal of *individual* human beings.

Eager longing

If history has a goal, life has meaning. Next, therefore, we consider the resurrection and everyday life. Like private religion —bearing down on one part of the whole—we condense the resurrection to but one moment—the last breath. But Paul says the resurrection gives an *overall* confidence in God's help and favor. He will give us "all things with him." In tribulation the list begins and continues with distress, persecution, famine, nakedness, peril, sword, and "anything else in all creation"—none of it can separate us from God's love expressed in the cross and the resurrection. We may "groan inwardly" but "God works for good with those who love him, who are called according to his purpose" [Rom. 8:28]. Out of our own crucified hopes come new hopes. We have the "first fruits of the Spirit," who helps us in our weakness. Despising this life and its joy is not a greater act of faith than accepting them. Of course we can absolutize our citizenship on earth and cram eternity into a lifetime. At the same time, we are just as capable of denying life and becoming lifeless beings, as if we had no hope. Resurrection is not escape; it is "eager longing." An old tale relates how a man preparing for eternity gave up all earthly joy and pleasure for paradise. He died. He entered the heavenly city. After two days, however, he left. He did not understand what was going on. God wants us to have life, and to have it abundantly. But there is no abundance if we bind ourselves to new chains, hide from life, and curse the darkness. Freud outlined palliative measures which are normal in times of trouble: (1) "powerful deflections" through which we make light of our misery, (2) "substitutive satisfactions" through which we diminish misery, (3) "intoxicating substances" through which we become insensitive to misery. But we cannot understand the full life, paradise itself, if we make light of, diminish, or become insensitive to this life. Whether our crucified hopes be divorce, cancer, the untimely death of a child, or failure, we understand them to be the strange germinating seeds for hope that does not disappoint. "If a way to the better there be," said Thomas Hardy, "it lies in taking a full look at the worst." To be sure, as Paul mentions, "the sufferings of this present time are not worth comparing with the glory that is to be revealed." And yet, if we are to be "fellow heirs with Christ" we must "suffer with him in order that we may also be glorified with him." The resurrection gives us hope for life now as well as later. Hence Luther could remark: "If I knew that tomorrow the world was going to end, I would want all the same to pay my debts and plant my little apple tree today." [1] Hope may not make things better, but it can make things bearable. Our hope lies with the *crucified* Jesus. God achieves victory by suffering, not by power. And God raises us up out of the ashes of sin and suffering to forgiveness and hope.

Nietzsche, however, derided the Christianity that flees reality and rushes to eternity. He presented an alternative:

I entreat you, my brothers, remain true to the earth, and do not believe those who speak to you of superterrestrial hopes! . . . They are despisers of life, atrophying and self-poisoned men, of whom the earth is weary: so let them be gone! Once blasphemy against God was the greatest blasphemy, but God died. . . . To blaspheme the earth is now the most dreadful offence.[2]

His derision is appropriate as far as one-eyed resurrection viewers consider the issue. We do not receive heaven at the expense of earth. We can say both yes and no, to die in part and survive in part. For suffering and death are paths to everlasting life. We are in the valley of the shadow of death, and of despair, waiting nevertheless in complete faith for resurrection to follow in our own experience.

Listen to Paul describe the exemplar of faith—Abraham:

In hope he believed against hope, that he should become the father of many nations; as he had been told, "So shall your descendants be." He did not weaken in faith when he considered his own body, which was as good as dead because he was about a hundred years old, or when he considered the barrenness of Sarah's womb. No distrust made him waiver concerning the promise of God, but he grew strong in his faith as he gave glory to God (Rom. 4:18-20).

Feasting and marching

Finally we must guard against the religious quacks, who would have us believe that life is not "crucial" in the sense that a cross lies in the center of life. Our life contains perpetual pain as we wrestle with conflicting claims, contradictions, and paradoxes. The quacks offer short cuts and time-saving methods on the road to victory. At one time the church contested the Gnostics who substituted "diversion of the brain for conversion of the heart." At other times the Church has done battle with those who confuse what we can know and what we can believe. Knowing is not presupposition for faith; rather, it is an element in faith. We do not hope, Paul says, for what we see. God is promise, never a formula. We rejoice in and praise the living

God who loves. He is not a bloodless concept. No one can look to God as he would look at an object. God reveals his glory "in the face of Christ." God looks at us. God looked at us even before we ever opened our mouths or our eyes. The resurrection is God's look at life and his seeing to it that nothing divides us from his love—neither sin nor trouble. We need to know only that "God is for us." The only understanding necessary is that we are fully understood. We are awaiting the revealing of the sons of God, when in full glory we will see him as he is. For now, "let us draw near with a true heart in full assurance of faith. . . . Let us hold fast the confession of our hope without wavering, for he who promised is faithful" (Heb. 10:22-23). Shout for joy! Raise the rooftop! "For the promise is to you and to your children and to all that are far off, every one whom the Lord our God calls to him" [Acts 2:39]. Shower-stall baritones get ready! Happy-hour monotones get ready! This is the feast of victory for our God! His truth goes marching on—now and tomorrow—Glory, glory, hallelujah!

NOTES

Introduction

1. *Luther's Works,* American Edition (hereafter cited as AE), vol. 31, pp. 40-41.
2. *Weimarer Ausgabe* 5, 179, 31
3. *Luther's Theology of the Cross* (Minneapolis: Augsburg, 1976), p. 18.
4. AE 25, 364-365
5. Althaus, Paul, *The Theology of Martin Luther* (Philadelphia: Fortress, 1966), p. 43.
6. AE 21, 340

Lent 1

1. Quoted by H. G. Haile in *Luther* (Garden City: Doubleday, 1980), p. 203.
2. *Ibid.*
3. Cited by William D. Streng in *In Search of Ultimates* (Minneapolis: Augsburg, 1969), p. 132.
4. Cited by Althaus in *The Theology of Martin Luther,* p. 292.
5. *Does God Exist?* (Garden City: Doubleday, 1980), p. 674.

Lent 2

1. *Preaching Law and Gospel* (Philadelphia: Fortress, 1978), p. 89.
2. *Wishful Thinking* (New York: Harper & Row, 1973), p. 28.

Lent 3

1. AE 21, 301
2. AE 21, 302
3. AE 21, 299
4. AE 21, 313
5. AE 21, 307
6. *Ibid.*

Lent 4

1. *Partners,* vol. 1, no. 3, p. 9.
2. *AE* 31, 55
3. *All the Damned Angels* (New York: Pilgrim, 1972), p. 112.

Lent 5

1. AE 51, 129-130
2. AE 21, 340

Maundy Thursday

1. *Tischreden* 3, 389-390
2. *Luther's World of Thought* (St. Louis: Concordia, 1965), p. 73.
3. *A Certain World* (New York: Viking, 1970), p. 150.
4. AE 31, 53
5. *Katallagete,* Winter 1974, pp. 25-26.

Good Friday

1. *A Certain World* (New York: Viking, 1970), p. 168.
2. *Katallagete,* Fall 1980, p. 13.
3. *Pilgrim at Tinker Creek* (New York: Bantam, 1974), p. 277.
4. *A Season in Hell* (New York: Pocket, 1977), p. 15.
5. AE 14, 31

Easter

1. Cited by Gerald O'Collins in *Man and His New Hopes* (New York: Herder and Herder, 1969), p. 167.
2. *Thus Spoke Zarathustra* (New York: Penguin, 1961), p. 42.

THE THEOLOGY OF THE CROSS
IN RESPONSIVE READINGS

- The following responsive readings, based on biblical sources, illuminate and heighten the theology of the cross.

- The preceding nine presentations are correlated with these responsive readings (see the table of contents).

LENT 1

THE CONSOLATION OF THE PSALTER—A

Pastor: My heart throbs, my strength fails me; and the light of my eyes—it also has gone from me. My friends and companions stand aloof from my plague, and my kinsmen stand afar off (Ps. 38:10-11).

People: For with thee is the fountain of life; in thy light do we see light (Ps. 36:9).

Pastor: Hear my prayer, O God; give ear to the words of my mouth. For insolent men have risen against me, ruthless men seek my life; they do not set God before them (Ps. 54:2-3).

People: The Lord is my light and my salvation; whom shall I fear? The Lord is the stronghold of my life; of whom shall I be afraid? (Ps. 27:1)

Pastor: For I know my transgressions, and my sin is ever before me. Against thee, thee only, have I sinned, and done that which is evil in thy sight, so that thou art justified in thy sentence and blameless in thy judgment. Behold, I was brought forth in iniquity, and in sin did my mother conceive me (Ps. 51:3-5).

People: But I have trusted in thy steadfast love; my heart shall rejoice in thy salvation (Ps. 13:5).

Pastor: Let them be put to shame and confusion who seek my life! Let them be turned back and brought to dishonor who desire my hurt! Let them be appalled because of their shame who say, "Aha, Aha!" (Ps. 70:2-3)

People: For he will give his angels charge of you to guard you in all your ways (Ps. 91:11).

Pastor: How long will you judge unjustly and show partiality to the wicked? Give justice to the weak and the fatherless; maintain the right of the afflicted and the destitute. Rescue the weak and the needy; deliver them from the hand of the wicked (Ps. 82:2-4).

People: And they shall sing of the ways of the Lord, for great is the glory of the Lord. For though the Lord is high, he regards the lowly; but the haughty he knows from afar (Ps. 138:5-6).

Pastor: Incline thy ear, O Lord, and answer me, for I am poor and needy (Ps. 86:1).

People: For the needy shall not always be forgotten, and the hope of the poor shall not perish for ever (Ps. 9:18).

Pastor: O God, why dost thou cast us off for ever? Why does thy anger smoke against the sheep of thy pasture? (Ps. 74:1)

People: For his anger is but for a moment, and his favor is for a lifetime. Weeping may tarry for the night, but joy comes with the morning (Ps. 30:5).

LENT 2

THE CONSOLATION OF THE PSALTER—B

Pastor: Be gracious to me, O Lord, for I am languishing; O Lord, heal me, for my bones are troubled. My soul also is sorely troubled. But thou, O Lord—how long? (Ps. 6:2-3)

People: Wait for the Lord; be strong, and let your heart take courage; yea, wait for the Lord! (Ps. 27:14)

Pastor: Why dost thou stand afar off, O Lord? Why dost thou hide thyself in times of trouble? (Ps. 10:1)

People: God is our refuge and strength, a very present help in trouble (Ps. 46:1).

Pastor: Turn thou to me, and be gracious to me; for I am lonely and afflicted. Relieve the troubles of my heart, and bring me out of my distresses. Consider my affliction and my trouble, and forgive all my sins (Ps. 25:16-18).

People: But I trust in thee, O Lord, I say, "Thou art my God." My times are in thy hand; deliver me from the hand of my enemies and persecutors! Let thy face shine on thy servant; save me in thy steadfast love! (Ps. 31:14-16)

Pastor: In my distress I called upon the Lord; to my God I cried for help. From his temple he heard my voice, and my cry to him reached his ears (Ps. 18:6).

People: Cast your burden on the Lord, and he will sustain you; he will never permit the righteous to be moved (Ps. 55: 22).

Pastor: My God, my God, why hast thou forsaken me? Why art thou so far from helping me, from the words of my groaning? O my God, I cry by day, but thou dost not answer; and by night, but find no rest (Ps. 22:1-2).

People: The Lord is gracious and merciful, slow to anger and abounding in steadfast love. The Lord is good to all, and his compassion is over all that he has made (Ps. 145:8-9).

Pastor: The snares of death encompassed me; the pangs of Sheol laid hold on me; I suffered distress and anguish (Ps. 116:3).

People: Even though I walk through the valley of the shadow of death, I fear no evil; for thou art with me; thy rod and thy staff, they comfort me (Ps. 23:4).

Pastor: Not to us, O Lord, not to us, but to thy name give glory, for the sake of thy steadfast love and thy faithfulness! (Ps. 115:1)

People: Blessed be his glorious name for ever; may his glory fill the whole earth! Amen and Amen! (Ps. 72:19)

LENT 3

THE CONSOLATION OF THE BEATITUDES

Pastor: Blessed are the poor in spirit, for theirs is the kingdom of heaven (Matt. 5:3).

People: He who is greatest among you shall be your servant; whoever exalts himself will be humbled, and whoever humbles himself will be exalted (Matt. 23:11-12).

Pastor: Blessed are those who mourn, for they shall be comforted (Matt. 5:4).

People: Blessed be the God and Father of our Lord Jesus Christ, the Father of mercies and God of all comfort, who comforts us in all our affliction, so that we may be able to comfort those who are in any affliction, with the comfort with which we ourselves are comforted by God. For as we share abundantly in Christ's sufferings, so through Christ we share abundantly in comfort too (2 Cor. 1:3-5).

Pastor: Blessed are the meek, for they shall inherit the earth (Matt. 5:5).

People: Love is patient and kind; love is not jealous or boastful; it is not arrogant or rude. Love does not insist on its own way; it is not irritable or resentful; it does not rejoice at wrong, but rejoices in the right. Love bears all things, believes all things, hopes all things, endures all things (1 Cor. 13:4-7).

Pastor: Blessed are those who hunger and thirst for righteousness, for they shall be satisfied (Matt. 5:6).

People: On the last day of the feast, the great day, Jesus stood up and proclaimed, "If any one thirst, let him come to me and drink. He who believes in me, as the scripture has said, 'Out of his heart shall flow rivers of living water'" (John 7:37-38).

Pastor: Blessed are the merciful, for they shall obtain mercy (Matt. 5:7).

People: Put on then, as God's chosen ones, holy and beloved, compassion, kindness, lowliness, meekness, and patience, forbearing one another and, if one has a complaint against another, forgiving each other; as the Lord has forgiven you, so you also must forgive. And above all these put on love, which binds everything together in perfect harmony (Col. 3:12-14).

Pastor: Blessed are the pure in heart, for they shall see God (Matt. 5:8).

People: For the grace of God has appeared for the salvation of all men, training us to renounce irreligion and worldly passions, and to live sober, upright, and godly lives in this world, awaiting our blessed hope, the appearing of the glory of our great God and Savior Jesus Christ, who gave himself for us to redeem us from all iniquity and to purify for himself a people of his own who are zealous for good deeds (Titus 2:11-14).

Pastor: Blessed are the peacemakers, for they shall be called sons of God (Matt. 5:9).

People: But now in Christ Jesus you who once were far off have been brought near in the blood of Christ. For he is our peace, who has made us both one, and has broken down the dividing wall of hostility, by abolishing in his flesh the law of commandments and ordinances, that he might create in himself one new man in place of the two, so making peace . . . (Eph. 2:13-15).

Pastor: Blessed are those who are persecuted for righteousness' sake, for theirs is the kingdom of heaven (Matt. 5:10).

People: For one is approved if, mindful of God, he endures pain while suffering unjustly. For what credit is it, if when you do wrong and are beaten for it you take it patiently? But if when you do right and suffer for it you take it patiently, you have God's approval. For to this you have been called, because Christ also suffered for you, leaving you an example, that you should follow in his steps (1 Peter 2:19-21).

LENT 4

THE CONSOLATION OF ISAIAH

Pastor: Sing for joy, O heavens, and exult, O earth; break forth, O mountains, into singing! For the Lord has comforted his people, and will have compassion on his afflicted (Isa. 49:13).

People: Fear not, for I am with you, be not dismayed, for I am your God; I will strengthen you, I will help you, I will uphold you with my victorious right hand (Isa. 41:10).

Pastor: All these things my hand has made, and so all these things are mine, says the Lord. But this is the man to whom I will look, he that is humble and contrite in spirit, and trembles at my word (Isa. 66:2).

People: Can a woman forget her sucking child, that she should have no compassion on the son of her womb? Even these may forget, yet I will not forget you. Behold, I have graven you on the palms of my hands; your walls are continually before me (Isa. 49:15-16).

Pastor: When the poor and needy seek water, and there is none, and their tongue is parched with thirst, I the Lord will answer them, I the God of Israel will not forsake them (Isa. 41:17).

People: But they who wait for the Lord shall renew their strength, they shall mount up with wings like eagles, they shall run and not be weary, they shall walk and not faint (Isa. 40:31).

Pastor: Behold, I am doing a new thing; now it springs forth, do you not perceive it? I will make a way in the wilderness and rivers in the desert (Isa. 43:19).

People: I have swept away your transgressions like a cloud, and your sins like mist; return to me, for I have redeemed you (Isa. 44:22).

LENT 5

THE CONSOLATION OF THE APOSTLE JOHN

Pastor: For God so loved the world that he gave his only Son, that whoever believes in him should not perish but have eternal life. For God sent the Son into the world, not to condemn the world, but that the world might be saved through him (John 3:16-17).

People: But to all who received him, who believed in his name, he gave power to become children of God (John 1:12).

Pastor: Again Jesus spoke to them, saying, "I am the light of the world; he who follows me will not walk in darkness, but will have the light of life" (John 8:12).

People: Jesus said to them, "The light is with you for a little longer. Walk while you have the light, lest the darkness overtake you; he who walks in the darkness does not know where he goes. While you have the light, believe in the light, that you may become sons of light" (John 12:35-36).

Pastor: How can you believe, who receive glory from one another and do not seek the glory that comes from the only God? (John 5:44)

People: Jesus answered, "If I glorify myself, my glory is nothing; it is my Father who glorifies me, of whom you say that he is your God (John 8:54).

Pastor: Let not your hearts be troubled; believe in God, believe also in me (John 14:1).

People: I am the good shepherd. The good shepherd lays down his life for the sheep (John 10:11).

Pastor: Peace I leave with you; my peace I give to you; not as the world gives do I give to you. Let not your hearts be troubled, neither let them be afraid (John 14:27).

People: My sheep hear my voice, and I know them, and they follow me; and I give them eternal life, and they shall never perish, and no one shall snatch them out of my hand (John 10:27-28).

Pastor: No one has ever seen God; the only Son, who is in the bosom of the Father, he has made him known (John 1:18).

People: Thomas said to him, "Lord, we do not know where you are going; how can we know the way?" Jesus said to him, "I am the way, and the truth, and the life; no one comes to the Father, but by me. If you had known me, you would have known my Father also; henceforth you know him and have seen him" (John 14:5-7).

Pastor: Simon Peter answered him, "Lord, to whom shall we go? You have the words of eternal life; and we have believed, and have come to know, that you are the Holy One of God" (John 6:68-69).

People: Jesus answered him, "If a man loves me, he will keep my word, and my Father will love him, and we will come to him and make our home with him (John 14:23).

Pastor: And the Word became flesh and dwelt among us, full of grace and truth; we have beheld his glory, glory as of the only Son from the Father (John 1:14).

People: When he had gone out, Jesus said, "Now is the Son of man glorified, and in him God is glorified; if God is glorified in him, God will also glorify him in himself, and glorify him at once (John 13:31-32).

Pastor: Jesus, knowing that the Father had given all things into his hands, and that he had come from God and was going to God, rose from supper, laid aside his garments, and girded himself with a towel. Then he poured water into a basin, and began to wash the disciples' feet, and to wipe them with the towel with which he was girded (John 13:3-5).

People: By this all men will know that you are my disciples, if you have love for one another (John 13:35).

THE CONSOLATION OF
THE LEAST OF ALL THE APOSTLES

Pastor: For I decided to know nothing among you except Jesus Christ and him crucified (1 Cor. 2:2).

People: For you know the grace of our Lord Jesus Christ, that though he was rich, yet for your sake he became poor, so that by his poverty you might become rich (2 Cor. 8:9).

Pastor: While we were yet helpless, at the right time Christ died for the ungodly. But God shows his love for us in that while we were yet sinners Christ died for us. (Rom. 5:6, 8).

People: For I am sure that neither death, nor life, nor angels, nor principalities, nor things present, nor things to come, nor powers, nor height, nor depth, nor anything else in all creation, will be able to separate us from the love of God in Christ Jesus our Lord (Rom. 8:38-39).

Pastor: For I through the law died to the law, that I might live to God. I have been crucified with Christ; it is no longer I who live, but Christ who lives in me; and the life I now live in the flesh I live by faith in the Son of God, who loved me and gave himself for me (Gal. 2:19-20).

People: For freedom Christ has set us free; stand fast therefore, and do not submit again to a yoke of slavery (Gal. 5:1).

Pastor: For by grace you have been saved through faith; and this is not your own doing, it is the gift of God—not because of works, lest any man should boast (Eph. 2:8-9).

People: He destined us in love to be his sons through Jesus Christ, according to the purpose of his will, to the praise of his glorious grace which he freely bestowed on us in the Beloved. In him we have redemption through his blood, the forgiveness of our trespasses, according to the riches of his grace which he lavished upon us (Eph. 1:5-8).

Pastor: And the peace of God, which passes all understanding, will keep your hearts and your minds in Christ Jesus (Phil. 4:7).

People: I can do all things in him who strengthens me (Phil. 4:13).

MAUNDY THURSDAY

THE GREAT REMEMBRANCES

Pastor: I set my bow in the cloud, and it shall be a sign of the covenant between me and the earth. When I bring clouds over the earth and the bow is seen in the clouds, I will remember my covenant which is between me and you and every living creature of all flesh; and the waters shall never again become a flood to destroy all flesh (Gen. 9: 13-15).

People: As a father pities his children, so the Lord pities those who fear him. For he knows our frame; he remembers that we are dust (Ps. 103:13-14).

Pastor: Remember not the sins of my youth, or my transgressions; according to thy steadfast love remember me, for thy goodness' sake, O Lord! (Ps. 25:7)

People: Yet I will remember my covenant with you in the days of your youth, and I will establish with you an everlasting covenant (Ezek. 16:60).

Pastor: In the course of those many days the king of Egypt died. And the people of Israel groaned under their bondage, and cried out for help, and their cry under bondage came up to God. And God heard their groaning, and God remembered his covenant with Abraham, with Isaac, and with Jacob (Exod. 2:23-24).

People: The Lord has made known his victory, he has revealed his vindication in the sight of the nations. He has remembered his steadfast love and faithfulness to the house of Israel (Ps. 98:2-3).

Pastor: Behold, the days are coming, says the Lord, when I will make a new covenant with the house of Israel and the house of Judah, not like the covenant which I made with their fathers when I took them by the hand to bring them out of the land of Egypt, my covenant which they broke, though I was their husband, says the Lord. But this is the covenant which I will make with the house of Israel after those days, says the Lord: I will put my law within them, and I will write it upon their hearts; and I will be their God, and they shall be my people. And no longer shall each man teach his neighbor and each his brother, saying, "Know the Lord," for they shall all know me, from the least of them to the greatest, says the Lord; for I will forgive their iniquity, and I will remember their sin no more (Jer. 31:31-34).

People: But the Counselor, the Holy Spirit, whom the Father will send in my name, he will teach you all things, and bring to your remembrance all that I have said to you (John 14:26).

Pastor: When my soul fainted within me, I remembered the Lord; and my prayer came to thee, into thy holy temple (Jon. 2:7).

People: Remember thy word to thy servant, in which thou hast made me hope. This is my comfort in my affliction that thy promise gives me life (Ps. 119:49-50).

Pastor: And he said, "Jesus, remember me when you come into your kingdom" (Luke 23:42).

People: Remember Jesus Christ, risen from the dead, descended

119

from David, as preached in my gospel, the gospel for which I am suffering and wearing fetters like a criminal. But the word of God is not fettered. Therefore I endure everything for the sake of the elect, that they also may obtain salvation in Christ Jesus with its eternal glory (2 Tim. 2:8-10).

Pastor: And when he had given thanks, he broke it, and said, "This is my body which is for you. Do this in remembrance of me." In the same way also the cup, after supper, saying, "This cup is the new covenant in my blood. Do this, as often as you drink it, in remembrance of me" (1 Cor. 11:24-25).

People: Let us draw near with a true heart in full assurance of faith, with our hearts sprinkled clean from an evil conscience and our bodies washed with pure water. Let us hold fast the confession of our hope without wavering, for he who promised is faithful; and let us consider how to stir up one another to love and good works, not neglecting to meet together, as is the habit of some, but encouraging one another, and all the more as you see the Day drawing near (Heb. 10:22-25).

GOOD FRIDAY

CREED OF THE CROSS

Pastor: He who loves father or mother more than me is not worthy of me; and he who loves son or daughter more than me is not worthy of me; and he who does not take his cross and follow me is not worthy of me. He who finds his life will lose it, and he who loses his life for my sake will find it (Matt. 10:37-39).

People: And being found in human form he humbled himself and became obedient unto death, even death on a cross. Therefore God has highly exalted him and bestowed on him the name which is above every name, that at the name of Jesus every knee should bow, in heaven and on earth and under the earth, and every tongue confess that Jesus Christ is Lord, to the glory of God the Father (Phil. 2:8-11).

Pastor: You know that after two days the Passover is coming, and the Son of man will be delivered up to be crucified (Matt. 26:2).

People: He himself bore our sins in his body on the tree, that we might die to sin and live to righteousness. By his wounds you have been healed. For you were straying like sheep, but have now returned to the Shepherd and Guardian of your souls (1 Peter 2:24-25).

Pastor: So they took Jesus, and he went out, bearing his own cross, to the place called the place of a skull, which is called in Hebrew Gol'gotha. There they crucified him, and with him two others, one on either side, and Jesus between them (John 19:17-18).

People: Looking to Jesus the pioneer and perfecter of our faith, who for the joy that was set before him endured the cross, despising the shame, and is seated at the right hand of the throne of God (Heb. 12:2).

Pastor: Christ redeemed us from the curse of the law, having become a curse for us—for it is written, "Cursed be every one who hangs on a tree" (Gal. 3:13).

People: The God of our fathers raised Jesus whom you killed by hanging him on a tree. God exalted him at his right hand as Leader and Savior, to give repentance to Israel and forgiveness of sins (Acts 5:30-31).

Pastor: For he was crucified in weakness, but lives by the power of God. For we are weak in him, but in dealing with you we shall live with him by the power of God (2 Cor. 13:4).

People: For Jews demand signs and Greeks seek wisdom, but we preach Christ crucified, a stumbling block to Jews and folly to Gentiles, but to those who are called, both Jews and Greeks, Christ the power of God and the wisdom of God (2 Cor. 1:22-24).

Pastor: For the word of the cross is folly to those who are perishing, but to us who are being saved it is the power of God (1 Cor. 1:18).

People: But now in Christ Jesus you who once were far off have been brought near in the blood of Christ. For he is our peace, who has made us both one, and has broken down the dividing wall of hostility, by abolishing in his flesh the law of commandments and ordinances, that he might create in himself one new man in place of the two, so making peace, and might reconcile us both to God in one body through the cross, thereby bringing the hostility to an end. . . . So then you are no longer strangers and sojourners, but you are fellow citizens with the saints and members of the household of God (Eph. 2:13-16, 19).

Pastor: Let all the house of Israel therefore know assuredly that God has made him both Lord and Christ, this Jesus whom you crucified (Acts 2:36).

People: But far be it from me to glory except in the cross of our Lord Jesus Christ, by which the world has been crucified to me, and I to the world (Gal. 6:14).

All: Humble yourselves therefore under the mighty hand of God, that in due time he may exalt you. Cast all your anxieties on him, for he cares about you. Be sober, be watchful. Your adversary the devil prowls around like a roaring lion, seeking some one to devour. Resist him, firm in your faith, knowing that the same experience of suffering is required of your brotherhood throughout the world. And after you have suffered a little while, the God of all grace, who has called you to his eternal glory in Christ, will himself restore, establish, and strengthen you. To him be the dominion for ever and ever. Amen (1 Peter 5:6-11).

EASTER

CREED OF THE RESURRECTION

Pastor: Truly, truly, I say to you, unless a grain of wheat falls into the earth and dies, it remains alone; but if it dies, it bears much fruit (John 12:24).

People: You were buried with him in baptism, in which you were also raised with him through faith in the working of God, who raised him from the dead (Col. 2:12).

Pastor: But we would not have you ignorant, brethren, concerning those who are asleep, that you may not grieve as others do who have no hope (1 Thess. 4:13).

People: For since we believe that Jesus died and rose again, even so, through Jesus, God will bring with him those who have fallen asleep (1 Thess. 4:14).

Pastor: If for this life only we have hoped in Christ, we are of all men most to be pitied (1 Cor. 15:19).

People: In my Father's house are many rooms (John 14:2).

Pastor: (Christ) will change our lowly body to be like his glorious body, by the power which enables him even to subject all things to himself (Phil. 3:21).

People: This is the will of him who sent me, that I should lose nothing at all that he has given me, but raise it up at the last day (John 6:39).

Pastor: And when I go and prepare a place for you, I will come again and will take you to myself, that where I am you may be also (John 14:3).

People: God raised the Lord and will also raise us up by his power (1 Cor. 6:14).

Pastor: I have suffered the loss of all things, and count them as refuse, in order that I may gain Christ . . . that I may know him and the power of his resurrection, and may share his sufferings, becoming like him in his death (Phil. 3:8, 10).

People: Just as we have borne the image of the man of dust, we shall also bear the image of the man of heaven (1 Cor. 15:49).

Pastor: If we have died with him, we shall also live with him (2 Tim. 2:11).

People: For as in Adam all die, so also in Christ shall all be made alive (1 Cor. 15:22).

Pastor: I consider that the sufferings of this present time are not worth comparing with the glory that is to be revealed to us (Rom. 8:18).

People: Beloved, we are God's children now; it does not yet appear what we shall be, but we know that when he appears we shall be like him, for we shall see him as he is (1 John 3:2).

Pastor: Your life is hid with Christ in God. When Christ who is our life appears, then you also will appear with him in glory (Col. 3:3-4).

People: We look not to the things that are seen but to the things that are unseen; for the things that are seen are transient, but the things that are unseen are eternal (2 Cor. 4:18).

Pastor: They shall see his face, and his name shall be on their foreheads (Rev. 22:4).

People: Now we see in a mirror dimly, but then face to face (1 Cor. 13:12).

Pastor: What no eye has seen, nor ear heard, nor the heart of man conceived . . . God has prepared for those who love him (1 Cor. 2:9).

People: We walk by faith, not by sight (2 Cor. 5:7).

Pastor: Then I saw a new heaven and a new earth; for the first heaven and the first earth had passed away (Rev. 21:1).

People: I saw the holy city, new Jerusalem, coming down out of heaven from God, prepared as a bride adorned for her husband (Rev. 21:2).

Pastor: But according to his promise we wait for new heavens and a new earth in which righteousness dwells (2 Peter 3:13).

People: For here we have no lasting city, but we seek the city which is to come (Heb. 13:14).

Pastor: He will wipe away every tear from their eyes, and death shall be no more, neither shall there be mourning nor crying nor pain any more (Rev. 21:4).

People: Thanks be to God, who gives us the victory through our Lord Jesus Christ (1 Cor. 15:57).

ADDITIONAL BIBLICAL REFERENCES

Genesis 45
Exod. 34:6
Deut. 21:23
Ps. 6:2-7
Ps. 55:2-5
Ps. 103:8-14
Ps. 149:4
Isa. 45:15
Isa. 49:13
Isa. 66:2
Matt. 8:16-17
Mark 8:34-35
Luke 24:25-26
John 1:14, 18
John 14:6, 7
Rom. 1:19-23
Rom. 6:3
Rom. 7:9-10

1 Cor. 2:2-10
1 Cor. 13:9-13
2 Cor. 5:10
Gal. 3:13
Gal. 6:14
Heb. 5:7
Heb. 6:13-20
Heb. 10:35-39
Hebrews 11
Heb. 12:3-5
Heb. 12:12-17
Heb. 13:12-16
James 4:6-10
1 Peter 5:6-11
1 John 2:9-11
Rev. 5:11-14
Rev. 21:22-27
Rev. 22:3-5

FOR FURTHER READING

Althaus, Paul. *The Theology of Martin Luther.* Philadelphia:
Fortress, 1966.

Bornkamm, Heinrich. *The Heart of Reformation Faith.* New
York: Harper & Row, 1965. Out of print.

Bornkamm, Heinrich. *Luther's World of Thought.* St. Louis:
Concordia, 1965.

Haile, H. G. *Luther.* Garden City: Doubleday, 1980.

Kadai, Heino O., ed. *Accents in Luther's Theology.* St. Louis:
Concordia, 1967. Out of print.

Koenker, Ernest B. *Great Dialecticians in Modern Christian
Thought.* Minneapolis: Augsburg, 1971. Out of print.

Loeschen, John R. *Wrestling with Luther.* St. Louis: Concordia,
1976.

Luther, Martin. *Luther's Works.* American edition. 56 vols.; esp.
vols. 21 and 31. St. Louis: Concordia; Philadelphia: Fortress.

Moltmann, Jürgen. *The Crucified God.* New York: Harper, 1974.

Steumpfle, Herman G. Jr. *Preaching Law and Gospel.* Philadelphia: Fortress, 1978.

Von Loewenich, Walther. *Luther's Theology of the Cross.* Minneapolis: Augsburg, 1976.

Watson, Philip S. *Let God Be God.* Philadelphia: Fortress, 1947.
Out of print.